<u>Notier'</u>

Maiden Voyage

The Prequel to The Adventure of a Lifetime

www.NotiersFrontiers.com

www.facebook.com/notiersfrontiers

www.instagram.com/timnotier

www.youtube.com/notiersfrontiers

Other Books by Notier's Frontiers Available on Amazon!

2Up and Overloaded

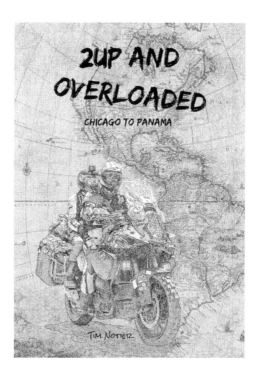

Maiden Voyage: The Prequel to The Adventure of a Lifetime introduced the characters, *2Up and Overloaded* sets them free into the world. Join Tim and his fiancée Marisa as they take a leap of faith and quit their jobs to circumnavigate the globe on their KTM 1190 Adventure motorcycle.

2Up and Overloaded is an inspiring, witty, sometimes-harrowing, and always gripping story, in which two people prepare extensively to explore the world on their motorcycle, only to discover that their most powerful resource can't be packed in a bag.

Coming Soon: Blood, Sweat, and Notiers

The adventure continues as Tim and Marisa explore the ruins and backroads of South America. They encounter difficult roads, friendliest people, and the most beautiful landscapes that they have come across on their journey to date. Ride along with them over muddy Peruvian mountain passes, through the mirrored splendor of the Bolivian Salt Flats, and navigate the wonders of Patagonia as they make their way to the *End of the World* in Ushuaia. A new cast of delightful characters accompany them along the way, enhancing Tim and Marisa's journey with friendship and some much-needed support. *Blood, Sweat, and Notiers* will leave you holding your breath in sections, cheering them on in others, and laughing all the way to end of the road.

To the love of my life, Marisa

They say opposites attract.
This point could not be proven finer,
Than the joining of the stars above,
Ursa Major and Ursa Minor.

Table of Contents

otier's
rontiers

Chapter 1 - One Bike, Two Bike; Orange Bike, Blue Bike

My 1900cc Yamaha Raider was my first true love. She was reliable and dependable; had been with me through thick and thin. She didn't complain, didn't consume much, or have any really bad habits. She had earned her place in my heart for the years of service and reliability she had provided.

I loved that bike so much I had it tattooed on the lower right side of my ribcage, so that I could forever proudly display my deep roots with my motorcycle. I had no intention of ever buying another bike.

But as much as I loved that bike, I loved Marisa, my girlfriend, more. Marisa has a wonderful sense of humor and a compassionate soul. I often tease her for having short-term memory, but that allows me to tell the same jokes over and over again, and each time I get that same genuine laugh.

Marisa was my high school sweetheart, and I was her prom date. After high school, she progressed into the next stage of her life and went to college. There was a ten-year break in our relationship, both of us following slightly different paths, hers much more interesting than mine.

She was given the chance to travel the world, including Australia, Guatemala, Jordan, China, and countless other destinations. She was able to dive into different cultures, making friends and memories along the way. She cared deeply for the many people around the world who had lives more difficult than our own. As she traveled, she learned what it truly meant to be compassionate, and exercises this knowledge as often as she can.

I, on the other hand, did not finish high school, but got a job, and after several years bought a house, a car, and a motorcycle, the whole time not venturing more than an hour away from the hospital I was born in. I was a semi-responsible, average American adult: working to live, living to work, drinking, watching football, and paying my taxes.

Our worlds collided every so often when Marisa would return home to visit her friends and family. She always had amazing stories to share but all she received in return was the same people telling different variations of the same stories while sitting in the same bars.

She pretended to enjoy these moments as kind people do, but I could only imagine she felt like she was looking into the wrong end of a telescope. Rather than the great vastness that can be explored outwardly, she was instead only able to focus on the minute life that had not changed since her last glimpse into the petri dish.

One day Marisa came home, and she was married. Completely unacceptable in my opinion. But in the events of her life, she had found someone who she believed she could live happily ever after with.

Her marriage did however bring her back to the U.S., back to Illinois, and back to our hometown, a mere twenty minutes away from where I lived. But as some relationships unfortunately discover, Marisa's happy ever after was not meant to be. As her marriage spiraled into divorce, I may have accidently-on-purpose bumped into her around town. Some crushes never go away.

Immediately after her divorce, Marisa moved into my apartment, where she is now, and forever will be by my side.

Marisa rode on the back of my Yamaha Raider throughout Illinois, Indiana, Michigan, Wisconsin, and across the Mississippi River into Iowa. On those trips, we tested the limits of both ourselves and the bike. We had to stop every hour or two for gas and so that Marisa's butt wouldn't turn black and blue from sitting on the passenger pillion—which would actually happen over the course of hours on the road.

What proved Marisa's unquestionable love for me was that while on these trips, because my bike had no sissy bar and little storage, she would have to carry our weekend's worth of travel supplies on her back.

This was not accomplished with the conventional I'm-going-to-school-with-some-books-and-a-lunch backpack. This was a fifty-year-old, sixty-gallon, actual Swiss Army straight-out-of-some-war-I'm-sure-I've-never-heard-of backpack. It had a steel frame and leather straps to tie down our sleeping bag. This huge bag, along with a bottle of Jack Daniels on top, was strapped to my five-foot-three, one-hundred-pound girlfriend without support for her back—that's love.

We enjoyed our mini adventures, but our extended weekend trips were not luxury cruises. These short expeditions were more like endurance tests until we arrived at our destination. As we began to plan more lengthy trips across the country, we quickly realized the Raider could not be our primary vehicle. We needed a better bike.

The spark to purchase an adventure motorcycle really started after I watched the documentary series *Long Way Round* and *Long Way Down*. That spark fanned into a flame as I read blogs and other forums about people who quit their jobs and sold their houses to travel the world on two wheels.

I watched Charlie and Ewan ride BMW adventure bikes across the globe, I read about Ted Simons riding a barely modified Triumph Cruiser, and even an article about a lovely lady doing the same on a pink scooter. It was obviously possible to ride around the world on an assortment of different vehicles, but of those three types of motorcycles, the adventure bike seemed best suited for us.

So I began the hunt for the perfect bike that would fill my new need for exploration via motorcycle. An "Adventure Bike" to me was one that not only had the ability to travel long distances of highway in comfort, but also had the capability of riding safely through the sections of the world not blessed with pristine pavement. After all, most adventures start where the road ends.

I didn't know much about adventure bikes, but at the time I knew that I needed a BMW 1200GSA because I had watched Ewan McGregor and Charley Boorman riding that exact bike on their journeys across the globe.

But after realizing that such a large impulse buy shouldn't be made purely by watching a television show, I decided to strategically research "Adventure Motorcycles" online, as any intelligent consumer should.

Typing in the words *adventure motorcycle* brought up countless miscellaneous websites, reviews, and comments about the same five motorcycles: the BMW 1200GSA, the Yamaha Super Tenere, the KTM 1190 Adventure, the Triumph Tiger, and the Ducati Multistrada. These posts were filled with individual descriptions detailing the pros and cons of the different bikes. Realistically, they were all awesome machines, but some of them fell short of the criteria I personally wished to have in a new, and no doubt expensive, adventure motorcycle.

The perfect bike had to meet two requirements: (1) it had to be well under 500 pounds, allowing full control and maneuverability while off-road, and (2) it had to have enough horsepower to carry two people with fully loaded panniers, and still be able to do eighty miles an hour with ease.

That mythical bike sadly did not exist. More horsepower meant more weight. There was no magic "adventure class" motorcycle that was both extremely light and had high horsepower. So I was forced to choose from the available options of actual manufactured motorcycles.

The general vibe on the forums was that the makers of the Multistrada most likely never intended this bike to do any serious off-roading. I knew that none of the potential bikes would be at the same caliber of off-roading as any motorcycle with an engine of 500cc or lower, but the Multistrada was the least capable of the five. It was not quite the adventure bike of my dreams, so I crossed it off my list.

Next, I looked at the 800cc Triumph Tiger, it was light and rugged, but not as powerful as some of the other options. If it was only me on the journey, 800cc would have been more than enough to get me to and through all of the places I wished to go. But, because I wanted to ride very long distances two up and fully loaded, this fell short in the power category.

The Super Tenere was a heavy, heavy beast, the heaviest of them all clocking in at a claimed wet weight of 584 lbs. Though I had the clearest of intentions to never drop the bike, I had seen enough people dropping their bikes going down very similar roads that I had imagined us going down. So I knew it was bound to happen, but then the problem would be picking the beast back up. The heavier weight also created handling issues in off-road conditions, which was a big negative for me. Thus, this heavyweight contender was knocked out in the third round, leaving two.

I know there are countless people who have one of the three bikes I eliminated, and they can rightfully state that their particular bike is the best in the class. But for each individual's preference, there are reasons behind their choice, and I had my own a process of elimination.

Finally it came down to either the BMW or the KTM as being the possible bike of my dreams. Germany vs. Austria.

There are hundreds of factors to calculate when choosing an adventure bike, but there are a few major factors that should take precedence to meet specific riding expectations. Both bikes are heavy, noted. Neither bike had a 21" front wheel that would allow for greater off-road maneuverability, noted.

I planned to do 90 percent of my riding two up on good old-fashioned tarmac for lengthy periods of time. I had no plans to zip down single-path dirt tracks, flying off jumps doing the superman as if practicing for the X Games.

I did, however, expect the bike to be capable of moderate off-road riding, through the back roads in Utah, Colorado, and any number of the potential trails off the beaten path.

Some of the roads of my dreams consisted of truly challenging terrain, especially for someone with as little experience as myself on this type of bike. I did not grow up with dirt bikes and had just a basic grasp of the off-road riding world. But as my experience would inevitably grow, I would have liked to have my bike's capabilities be patiently waiting for me to catch up.

A brand new shiny BMW 1200GSA was around twenty-two thousand American dollars plus tax. That was just um ... that was a lot of cash. The BMW had service intervals at every six thousand miles compared to KTM at every nine thousand miles. The KTM 1190 was much lighter and had more ground clearance than the Beamer. All of that was in addition to the fact that I just didn't have twenty-two thousand dollars, (I really didn't have sixteen thousand dollars either, but that was six thousand dollars *less* that I didn't have).

I took a quick glance at the BMW F800 Adventure, but the same initial reasoning behind not wanting an 800cc motorcycle popped back into my head. The difference in price between the 800cc BMW and the 1190cc KTM was not much at all. A final test ride between the F800 and KTM 1190 quickly announced the winner.

Choosing the manufacture felt simple in comparison to choosing the color of the bike. Orange or gray.

Orange? Or *Gray*?

This decision took an hour longer than it should have for any normal human being. There were a couple of swinging moments between making a confident decision and then instantly changing my mind.

"I really like the orange," I said to Robert, the salesman. Only seconds later I'd follow up this declaration with, "But the gray model looks pretty awesome too."

"Yup," was all he could say to my obvious internal struggle.

"Marisa, what do you think?" I asked.

"They're both very nice," she stated, knowing my question was more rhetorical than a request for input.

"Sorry, this has to be fairly annoying," I apologized repeatedly to Robert, realizing my inability to choose was taking half the day.

"Not at all, man, you're good," was what came out audibly, but his eyes were screaming, 'You have got to be kidding me! Orange or gray! Orange or friggin' gray!'

After at least another twenty minutes of pacing back and forth and looking the bikes over as if staring was going to change something, I finally chose a color to the delight of the very patient salesman. He half-doubtingly wrote down the serial number of the bike for the certificate of sale, and my color debate was finalized once and for all.

I was now the proud owner of a brand new gray KTM 1190 Adventure. I went with the gray model because the neutral color made the orange accents stand out on the body and the rear shock. That was my highly biased, but totally scientific reasoning anyway.

I realistically couldn't afford it, didn't have a very good use for it except a dream … but man, did I want it.

Chapter 2 - Go West, Young Man

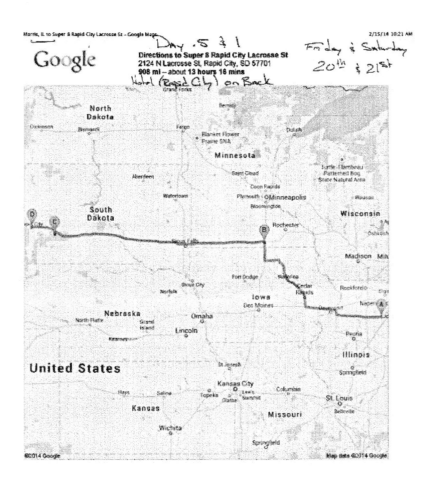

Now that we had the proper vehicle to shoot my love and myself into the unknown, it was time for some adventure practice. I wanted to paint a smaller picture to be sure I was up to the challenge of a much larger, full-on *Creation of Adam* devotion to my motorcycling endeavor. A maiden voyage, if you will.

Part of my agreement going into my current job was a negotiated nineteen vacation days in the summer. Marisa was a teacher, with summers off, so this worked out perfectly.

Marisa has travelled around the world, across countless countries, but had yet to explore the landmarks within our own borders. We agreed our first adventure would be a trip around the western states, following some of the same routes my father had taken my family in a packed minivan when I was a child. I thought it would be fun to create an itinerary to places burnt into my memory from days of old, and to places out west that the friendly online community suggested as must see.

Like my father had done for our family, it would be up to me to be the tour guide for Marisa. I created the itinerary and decided which destinations to fit into the nineteen days. I gained a new appreciation for my father's efforts as I spent days trying to balance the time it would take us to reach each waypoint while still leaving us with plenty of time to actually see the sights.

There were many rough drafts, each one adding certain destinations, removing others, changing the number of days spent at a particular place, and then revising things pretty much back to the original concept.

Nineteen days was both a lot of time, as well as not enough. It was a decent block of time to get some lengthy days in the saddle, but the number of possible places we could get to from Illinois and still allow ourselves the time to actually look around depleted nineteen days very quickly.

There were some destinations that would just have to wait until our next adventure. I would rather see more of fewer places than have to speed from one destination to another, zipping along from one rally point to the next. Absorption of the journey was very important, and I knew it was the key to building true memories to reflect on.

Marisa agreed very much on this matter, so I was glad she wasn't disappointed by not going to the Grand Canyon, a big point of interest for her. The Grand Canyon, Mesa Verde, and other amazing places gave us plenty of reasons to go back to the west in the future.

With our limited number of days, we both decided it might be best to trailer the bike to Rapid City, South Dakota. We could then leave the car and trailer behind, make our loop around the western states on the bike alone, and pick up the trailer on the way back home. This would allow us to drive much farther across the plains of the Midwest without having to stop for rest as often. As much as I disliked the idea of trailering the bike, it seemed with our time constraints to be the best possible option.

We would try to cover the 908 miles from Illinois to South Dakota in a little over thirteen hours of driving split between two days. The aim was to get to Rapid City early enough to find extended parking for the car and trailer, most likely at the Rapid City Airport. Once we ditched the car, we could backtrack to the Badlands, which was only an hour away. Then we could zoom around on the motorcycle, freeing her into the wild as she was bred to be.

Anyway, I figured we would have enough butt-on-seat time by riding in a huge circle around the Rocky Mountains, and didn't feel bad about driving through some of the less interesting scenery with the trailer. Between the two of us, we could share some of the responsibility of driving the car to get as far west as possible before stopping for the first night.

So with all of our preparations in place (that we thought to cover at the time), all that was left was to ride the KTM up a ramp onto the used trailer I bought online. It sounded simple enough, but driving up that ramp was one of the most uncomfortable things I've ever done.

I wanted a small trailer because I was using a Mazda 3 to pull its load. With that being said, it was an extremely small trailer. My KTM left about a half an inch of plywood behind her rear wheel, and just enough room on the left and right side to put my feet down.

To successfully get on top of the narrow, short trailer, I had to get enough speed to shoot up the ramp (two feet wide) and then slam on the brakes once aboard to slide the front wheel into the chock.

I had seen enough epic fails online on how *not* to do this. I watched plenty of people drop their bikes doing what I was about to do for the first time. Images of worst-case scenarios kept leaping to mind every time I lined the bike up, gunned it for four feet, only to stop just shy of the ramp.

The charade playing out in front of my house drew the attention of my neighbor, Hank, who lived across the street. Hank walked over, making me feel even less of a man, and evaluated the situation.

"There's really only one way to do it," Hank stated nonchalantly. "Just buckle up and go for the ride."

I, of course, could not buckle up, and was extremely terrified of the short ride ahead of me.

"All you have to do is follow through," Marisa said encouragingly.

Even with the toned-down Cliffs Notes so easily described by Hank, and the loving words of Marisa, it was a very frightening moment for me. And to make things worse, I now had spectators.

With my breath held, knowing I was making a much bigger deal out of the situation than necessary, and with the impression Marisa no longer cared to watch me not do it over and over again ... I gunned it, shot up the ramp in pure fear, hit the brakes, and smiled from ear to ear once I realized that all was well in the world.

If I had been in Marisa's situation, I would have already unpacked my stuff and made other plans for the extended vacation in the amount of time it took me to get up that ramp. She might have rolled her eyes while I wasn't looking, but she gleamed at me with satisfaction when I looked down at her from atop the first challenge of the trip.

We then strapped the bike down with six straps in a fashion that made the best logical sense to us. Not so loose that it would move around, not so tight that it would snap under too much pressure. This was one of many trial and error lessons to be learned on the trip because what we thought was secure, turned out not to be the case.

After all was fastened, we backed the car out of the driveway, and set off on our adventure to the west.

I immediately knew that Marisa, as good as her driving skills were, would not be sharing the driving responsibilities with the bike in tow as I had originally anticipated. This was only because if any of the horrible scenes that kept playing out in my mind of the bike falling off actually occurred, it would be better if they happened while I was behind the wheel. Then any blame would solely be on me.

Not ten miles into the trip, the first of numerous straps broke. We had spares, but I wasn't a hundred percent on the fundamental physics behind strapping a motorcycle down.

Securing an object with its own suspension was tricky for me. Tight seemed to be real tight. At the time, I understood the theory that if I hit a bump, the suspension would compress and then shoot back out, possibly snapping the strap. So I was trying to balance this against what I thought to be the maximum tension strength of the straps themselves.

Newbie lesson number one: you must tighten all the straps down as far as you humanly can to disallow any movement whatsoever. I didn't learn that lesson until the way home, after spending a hundred dollars on multiple variations of different straps that would have worked fine individually in the correct application and would all fail collectively when used incorrectly as I continuously and stubbornly chose.

I drove thirteen hours in constant fear and stress. I stared into the rear-view mirror and thought my motorcycle would fall off my trailer at every bump and turn, topple to the side, and end the trip before I had even unleashed her into the wilds of the west.

Thankfully, and despite the ever-constant strap breakage, my bike stayed on the trailer.

We pulled into a random hotel late in the evening once I believed I reached my limit of safe driving. This was well past the proposed stop for the night way back in Albert Lea, Minnesota, since I felt the urge to drive as far as possible to kick-start the trip. Now we were only three hours from Rapid City, South Dakota.

The KTM was safely parked atop her trailer for the night, with more dead bugs on her than all the sticky fly tape traps in Tennessee have ever caught. The day's extra credit miles of pushing onward left us exhausted, but we were that much closer to getting through the plains. We would rise early in the morning, drop off the car in Rapid City, ride back to the Badlands to explore, and then the mighty motorcycle journey would begin.

Chapter 3 - Good Omens and Badlands

When I stepped outside the next morning, the gods seemed to look down on my bike with good fortune. Rays of light pierced through the clouds with branching fingers of heaven in a kaleidoscope surrounding my bike. Marisa didn't recall it being that magical, but I hoped that it was a good omen that would carry throughout our trip.

We set back on the road with growing anticipation, knowing we would soon begin our adventure that we had planned so thoroughly. In just a few hours, the safety net of our car would be removed, and we would be riding around a very awesome part of the country.

But before we got to that amazing launching point of our journey, we had to make it through a stretch of Highway 90 plastered with billboards for Wall Drug. Usually I do not care or pay attention to the countless varieties of signs flying by, but it seemed that every fifty feet there was yet another billboard peddling five-cent coffee, or a ten-cent shave, and other visual spam. Hundreds of these signs polluted my peripheral vision with tacky sayings and quotations. Marisa and I couldn't help but comment on them, and those comments soon turned into complaints. Eventually, we vowed to never visit Wall Drug.

The plan for the day was to get to Rapid City and backtrack to the Badlands, but once the exit for the Badlands appeared in front of us, I couldn't stand passing it without pulling in. So we decided we would take the bike off the trailer, ride around the Badlands, and drive to Rapid City with me on the bike and Marisa in the car once the day's adventure was complete.

We pulled into a gas station at the entrance to the park and prepared to take the bike off the trailer. After we unbound the machine, I once again found myself sitting on the bike on the trailer with a familiar fear flowing through my veins. I would somehow have to wheel the bike backwards and down the ramp to the safety of solid ground.

This began yet another episode of me making a huge deal out of a fairly simple task. Marisa states that I do this often, and I have not given it much thought until I began recalling these moments. She may be correct about this trait in my character.

Sitting about two feet above the ground, with eight feet behind me in a reverse straightaway down to the earth, I found myself at a standstill. Marisa, knowing the drill, waited as I tried to will myself into moving.

"Maybe we could both walk it down on either side of the ramp," Marisa suggested, trying to solve the problem as a team.

I arrogantly threw her suggestion aside. I pictured myself losing the distribution of weight, and in one swift action, I would crush the two things I held dearest to my heart: my bike and my pride.

Once again, I drew enough attention to myself that a very friendly man came over and asked if he could assist.

"Looks like you folks could use a hand," said our new-found friend.

Between the three of us, and with me finally agreeing that walking it down would be best, we easily guided the bike backwards to the comfort of solid ground.

Thank God I would not need to ride up or down that ramp for weeks; my ego would not have been able to manage the embarrassment of the dependency on others for such a basic task. But now the bike, Marisa, and I were free at last.

With a full tank of gas, and the addition of a nice little fox tail that we purchased from the gift shop attached to the handlebars, Marisa and I hopped on and took off into the Badlands.

The Badlands were absolutely amazing, and very hot. With the help of continuous rain over the previous weeks, the majority of the landscape was filled with rich green grass. It looked like some twisted version of Ireland. Between the flat, lush plains shot up huge mounds of grey, brown, and red earth.

We pulled over immediately at the first side pull-off to stare at the spectacle before us. The parking lot was strategically located next to one of these giant formations that was large enough to climb around. So we proceeded to get "hands-on" with the scenery and dismounted.

The formations were like giant wasp nests or termite mounds, but the size of ten-story buildings. They were made of a mixture of mud, dirt, and rock that created a fairly erodible surface that we could pick away with our fingers.

Without much effort, we found our first "Oh my God" view of the trip as the mounds we were climbing on suddenly split into two peaks. (43.784783, -101.900227* GPS Coordinates) Walking out ten feet between the peaks led to a drop-off of a hundred feet or so. The elevated view of the landscape shooting out to the horizon was positively breathtaking.

We knew this was the first of many views that would leave us just staring into the bizarre scenery, so we looked at each other with a sort of giddy delight and without a word, ventured farther. We had only penetrated a mile or so into the park and knew we had made the right decision in coming here prior to Rapid City. Instead of backtracking, we were now able to spend more time roaming around carefree.

A long twisting road that weaved between these colorful mounds was our new interstate, while dirt and gravel roads branched out around us, beckoning us to sink our tires into them. Pull-offs on either side of the road led us to an intimate view of nature like no other.

We stared out at alien worlds plucked from old *Star Trek* episodes. Mounds rose out of the ground with no particular pattern or consistency. They were truly a magical phenomenon. Even with science and the forces of nature explained on small plaques, it was still hard to understand and absorb nature's raw beauty.

Colors burst from deep within the hills in different layers. The landscape looked as if it had measles. Small valleys and roads snaked their way around each hill, interconnecting and winding without care of direction or altitude. They wandered free and without regulation; I hoped that our journey would be as open to the countless possibilities as the roads that crisscrossed below.

Compelled by the unusual terrain, we pulled over time and time again. Every wondrous scene called out to us. We rode past a sign that read "Off-Road Vehicles Only," and that was all I needed to know that it was destined for me.

I turned down the rutted road, curious to find out if I would drop the bike the anticipated number of times I had calculated while riding down a road with water-filled tire tracks.

I dodged and weaved my way through a semi-solid patch of ground with tall grass running down the center. I stood up like a proud soldier going around fifteen to twenty miles per hour, successfully navigating Marisa and myself through some crappy terrain.

"This is awesome," I said.

"I was just thinking to myself how much this sucks," Marisa replied.

It turned out that the excitement of the crappy terrain was only enjoyed by me. Sitting on the back, Marisa had been absorbing the recoil from the various unseen trenches and ruts without warning.

We were also riding away from the more robust scenery. So, happy with my first experience of the trip that could technically be called off-roading, we reversed our course, and traveled back to the scenic byway to progress farther around the loop of the park.

The Badlands National Park's map showed an area where buffalo "roam". We headed towards this destination as Marisa was dying to see an actual buffalo.

And there they were, grazing right where the map stated they would be, in an area labeled Robert's Prairie Dog Town. The bison walked up to the edge of the road, drawing in a large crowd of people pulled over to get their photo ops with the huge creatures. We did the same and got our snapshots as we stared in awe.

I found it odd that these free-roaming bison had their own permanent spot on the map. Upon closer inspection into the landscape, I saw the smallest hints of a fence against the back end of the horizon. With a cliff on the other side of the road, it became clear that these buffalo were not as free as one would initially assume. They were still buffalo, though, and that was pretty awesome all by itself.

We moved down the road with a sense of accomplishment for what we had already experienced throughout the day. The sun continued to beat down on us. It was very hot, but I still wanted to trek around at least one of the paths that climbed up and around some of the larger colorful land masses that shot skyward.

We pulled into a parking lot to stretch before hiking up one of the trails. Climbing those beautiful bluffs felt like we were in a scene from *Young Guns*. Everything seemed surreal, and I was so ecstatic to be exactly where we were in that moment. I glanced over to see the look on Marisa's face suggesting she was in the same state of bliss that I was.

It took us the better part of thirty minutes to get to the top of the huge hill. The sun was out in full force, and we utilized any shade available for short breaks to catch our breath.

"You want to know a fun fact?" Marisa asked as we stood in the shade of some huge rocks.

"I love spur-of-the-moment fun facts," I replied.

"Well, just like us, rattlesnakes also tend to hang out in shaded areas to escape the sun's heat," she happily informed me.

"Well, I am ready to move on, you good?" I stated as my strength suddenly returned to me with the endurance to press forward.

We continued to climb and assumed that once we reached the top, there would be a grand view of the bluffs, only to find a flat plain of green grass at the top. The ups and downs, ins and outs, and breaks in the earth made it very tricky to guess what was just over the next peak, and at what elevation we would be.

While the sun beat directly down on us, the amount of perspiration that flowed out of our pores over the last couple of hours began to have a noticeable effect on us. We had not mounted the panniers on the bike yet and did not have water, another rookie mistake and a fairly dangerous one. Because of the heat, we figured we should make our way back to the gas station sooner than later.

We hiked back down the trail, got back on the bike, and followed the road to a T intersection. To the left was a gravel road that disappeared around a bend, turning and dipping into the landscape.

The second option to the right would lead back to the highway where we could complete our loop around the Badlands via the interstate back to the car. I opted for the gravel road.

We rode down into green fields and rock formations that we had previously viewed from the main road high above. Off the beaten path was an understatement as the road was not even marked on the map.

We did not see another soul for miles until we came upon a ranger on the side of the road and asked her where the road led. She stated it went far to the south to meet up with another highway many miles away. She was taking pictures of the blooming flowers on the hills. She said it was a rarity to see so much foliage and flowers in the Badlands, but this season had been particularly wet.

I could have traveled down that road that stretched and weaved into the south until my gas tank was empty, but we had a schedule to keep. This was only the first scenic destination, and it was proving to be a memorable experience already. We saw a small bridge in the distance and decided we would turn around when we got to the bridge.

Once we returned to the T intersection, the new choices were to go back the way we came through the park or make our way north to I-90 and head east to the gas station via a quicker route. Marisa and I thought it would be better to ride the more scenic southern loop, even if it added additional time.

It was a lovely ride back, so much to take in while still having to keep 80 percent of my concentration on the road ahead of me. An extra bonus that wasn't fully appreciated until the journey began was having Marisa as a dedicated cameraman who sat directly behind me. I would shout, "Get a picture of that," and, "Over to the right," while she had already done so twice, but would confirm my request with a thumbs up.

Once we got back to the car, we ran into the gas station to rehydrate and buy a few postcards for our families. It was a great day. The bike was off the trailer, we had a successful introduction to the west, and we were well on the way to an awesome adventure.

With the hotel's address plugged into the GPS in the car, Marisa led the way into Rapid City where we would spend the first and last nights of our Great Western Adventure. Our hope was to find a hotel that would allow us to leave the car and trailer in the parking lot. If not, we would have to drive it to the extended parking at the Rapid City Airport.

Once we arrived at the hotel we explained our circumstance to the lady checking us in, Vicki. She stated that two weeks was just too long to leave a car unattended in the parking lot. But in an act of kindness, she offered us her driveway just outside the city at no cost and peace of mind for our car's safety while we were on our travels. Vicki was getting off work soon so she could take us there, and we eagerly accepted her offer.

With only a couple of hours until we would be completely dependent on only the motorcycle and its luggage, Marisa and I unpacked the tent, camping gear, panniers, and everything else we would be taking on the bike. We carefully packed it all onto the KTM, making sure we did not leave anything necessary in the car.

Once we felt comfortable with the dressing of the motorcycle, we rendezvoused with Vicki, who was just finishing work. We met her in the parking lot and began to follow her to the house we would be abandoning our car at for the duration of our trip. Marisa drove the car, and I followed on the KTM.

Vicki lived about fifteen minutes northwest of downtown Rapid City in a house with a view that I could wake up to every day and be at peace. Her community lay at the bottom of one of the giant, forest covered hills that popped out of the landscape. Everywhere I looked, there was a breathtaking scene that could be taken in for hours.

I gave her some cash because I felt I should give her something for her generosity. Vicki tried to refuse politely, but I reminded her she was saving us a lot of money by not having to utilize the airport's extended parking. She was a good person and said the car would be safe.

Vicki wished us luck and a worry-free, wonderful trip. Then, we parted ways for the two weeks it would take to travel around the Rockies. Marisa jumped on the back of the KTM and we proceeded to ride back to the hotel, successfully having ditched the car.

Unknown to us at the time, our Mazda 3 had a magical ward that dispelled any collection of moisture in the air. But as we left it parked in a stranger's driveway far from home, it could no longer protect us from the elements. So as soon as we got back onto the highway, it began to rain.

Thinking we were just going on a short hop in and out of town, we did not have helmets or any of our fancy rain gear we had purchased just prior to leaving. This was another mistake in our lack of preparation, and now, we had to suffer the consequences. Needless to say, we were soaked within thirty seconds.

"Let's never get caught in the rain without our gear again," Marisa said frustrated.

"I know. I'm sorry," I replied.

A little fact about Marisa is that she hates being wet, and she hates being cold, and she absolutely despises being both at the same time.

We pulled over at the first gas station we came across to get something to eat and try to wait out the storm. After we accepted the fact we would not be getting back to the hotel dry, Marisa and I decided to just get on the bike and ride slowly towards town.

Like wet dogs we got off the bike and ran into the hotel to strip our soaked clothing off and jump into a hot shower. Once Marisa's body reached her average core temperature (I swear it is 78.6 degrees, she always seems to be around twenty degrees colder than everyone else), she crawled into bed.

I stood in the bathroom with the wall mounted hair-dryer trying to dry out my boots. At the same time, I checked the upcoming weather on my phone for the following day's travel through the Black Hills.

The next day's total was about 245 miles, with an estimated five hours of riding. The weather was not prime for motorcycling: precipitation with pockets of sun, but mostly rain and wet conditions. With the forces of nature out of our control and a schedule we needed to stick to, we went to sleep with a positive attitude, both of us very excited, despite the upcoming forecast of gloom and doom.

Chapter 4 - Rain, Check

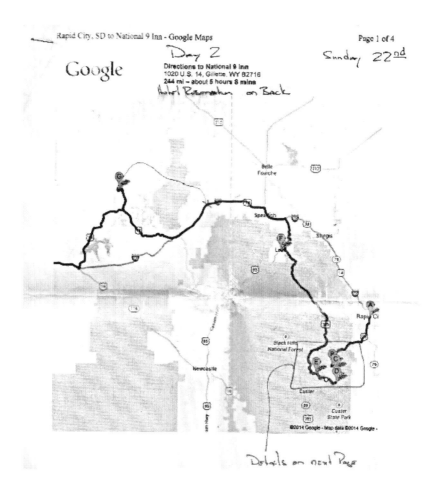

Google

Day 2

Sunday 22nd

Directions to National 9 Inn
1020 U.S. 14, Gillette, WY 82716
244 mi ~ about 5 hours 8 mins

Hotel Reservation on Back

Details on next Page

The next day we prepared for the worst by putting on our rain gear right off the bat. The amount of adrenaline that pumped through us outshined the overcast sky outside.

After eating a hearty breakfast, I downed as much coffee as I could, and we set out for our first full day on the motorcycle.

The plan was to ride around the beautiful roads that flowed through the heart of the Black Hills to Mount Rushmore and Needles Highway, then head back north towards the town of Lead, South

Dakota and stop for something to eat. After lunch, we would get back on US-90 West and head into Wyoming to see Devil's Tower and proceed to Gillette, Wyoming where we would sleep in a hotel for the night.

The roads of the Black Hills consisted of long, sweeping lines through majestic forests cut into the side of the hills. When significant climbs in elevation took place, we had to ride a cloverleaf ramp pitched at a steep angle that turned back in over itself via a bridge, then tunneled through the stone of the mountain. There were many of these tight-turning roller coaster climbs, and all were just as fun as the initial one.

As we approached a narrow, one-lane tunnel burrowing through the mountain, multiple stop signs and 'sound horn' notifications appeared. So, as recommended, with a heavy thumb I pressed the horn button. Nothing happened.

I hit it again, only to discover that it was not user error, but something had gone astray with either the wiring or a fuse. So I screamed, "BEEP BEEP!" as loud as I could and proceeded into the tunnel with caution. I thought to myself that if a broken horn were the only thing that would go wrong with my bike, then I would take it.

The crafty individuals who designed these roads had a couple of tricks up their sleeves for the wandering soul. Once close enough to do so, every other of the tight loop-back cloverleafs led to one of the single lane tunnels opening to a direct shot of Mount Rushmore on the other side. The trees were cut in a perfect row, clearing a straight view of the magnificent man-made structure.

As we continued to climb towards the national monument, Marisa and I saw marvelous views of the masterpiece as we traveled down the main road leading to the entrance of the park.

In the creation of the monument, it was said that no one would have to pay to see this national treasure. The views therefore, were free; the parking, however, was eleven dollars. We decided not to park and continued on to Needles Highway.

Needles was within the same area of the Black Hills and made yet more twists and turns that crawled up the side of the forest-covered hills. At the apex of the climb were views like something out of a fantasy movie. It looked to be the homeland of a dark sorcerer, and just as we reached the top of the hills, it began to rain.

Black pillars of stone rose into the sky like Titans' boney fingers reaching out of the ground toward the heavens. The rain fit the scenery perfectly. It felt like it should always be raining there. Even with the rain beating down on us, we pulled over to view the surroundings and to absorb the madness of the landscape.

We anticipated the rain, so we had our rain gear on. But we soon found out that even though this gear indeed worked better than the cheap, truck stop poncho-type rain suits we used to wear, our current setup was still not 100 percent waterproof. Water managed to find its way through some of the seams and seep through and dampen our clothing beneath.

I was armed with the addition of a garbage bag with holes cut out for my head and arms, because during a trial run in some light rain, I discovered that water tended to make a straight line through the zipper and Velcro chest portion.

I also figured out that utilizing rubber bands on the wrist cuffs stopped a healthy amount of water from flowing up the sleeves. Still, it was 99 percent better than the position we had found ourselves in the day prior, and though a little wet, our spirits were high and we pressed forward.

In the end, the small amounts of moisture collecting in various spots turned into large amounts of water collecting just about everywhere. We pulled over once again at a large hotel in the middle of one of the passes through the hills. We just needed to take a fresh, dry look at the map to confirm that we were going in the correct direction.

"This sucks," I said stubbornly.

Between the chattering of Marisa's teeth, she managed to say, "Agreed. Do you know where we're going?"

"Not a clue. This is the first time I have ever been here and the little squiggly line on the map doesn't provide very much detail of our exact location," I replied.

"We should be somewhere around here." Marisa pointed to the map. "So if we just continue heading north we should eventually hit Lead."

I decided to revise our route. Instead of going back north to the city of Lead, we would now ride south to Custer to eat lunch and get out of the rain for a bit, then continue west into Wyoming on US-16. This would allow us to avoid the highway miles from the northern route.

Marisa and I were slightly lost and soaked in some key areas, causing discomfort, and the thought of adding any extra miles to an already tedious ride was unappealing. My hands had pruned up from the constant exposure to water. I was a little upset with our current situation.

We took a few moments to shake off the rain and get our bearings before getting back on the bike to go in the direction we had just came in our pursuit of Custer, South Dakota.

While riding down from the tops of the Black Hills, we saw the signs we so desperately needed for Route 16 to Custer. The rain was getting worse, but there was nothing to do except aim the bike forward and proceed with caution. At least we knew we were headed in the right direction, and were making progress towards a hotel and dry clothes. Yet we also knew we weren't even halfway there.

Route 16 ran straight through Custer City and continued west, but we felt the need to push on because of the rain delays. So we decided to keep riding through and eat in a town farther down the road.

To our dismay, at the very end of Custer City limits, the very same Route 16 that was to be our salvation to getting us back on track to Wyoming, was under construction.

It was not the type of construction where one lane was closed and everyone had to merge and proceed slowly. This was the type of construction where they stripped the road down to bare earth before rebuilding with dirt and loose gravel.

Other motorcyclists had already turned around and were now flashing their lights at us and giving the universal turnaround sign with an imaginary lasso over their heads.

We indeed turned around to get a breakdown of the situation from a biker who was parked on the shoulder.

"I'd go back the other way if I were you," the female rider advised.

"Dammit, we just rode all the way down here as a shortcut," I replied.

"It's not bad at first, but it gets bad real quick," she warned. "You'll find yourself in ankle deep mud about a hundred yards up the road."

As much as I was up to off-roading, I knew of two conditions that my Conti Attack 2 tires did not score very high on. Wet mud and deep sand did not receive any five-star ratings for my tires, and this road sounded like it could have both.

"Dammit," I repeated.

She continued to forewarn us of the dangers ahead. "Our group figured we could make it, but six riders have gone down so far. So I said screw it and turned around. It's madness up there. People dropping their bikes, snapping off fairings, and bending crash bars. Not worth it, man."

Liquid mud had crawled up her legs to her knees, and she was visually shaken by what she had just gone through. We watched some of the eastbound traffic coming towards us, and by the look of their vehicles, it was clear it was a muddy stew ahead.

Given the choice, I stubbornly, but wisely, headed back towards Custer City and pulled over at the first diner we saw. I parked under a gazebo to shelter the bike from being assaulted by the relentless rain.

Marisa and I removed the layers of wet clothing and replaced them with dry counterparts. We watched more cars drive our direction from the west completely covered in sludge. I knew I had made the correct decision, even if it meant having to backtrack the entire way we had come, which was our original route anyway.

We headed into the diner for something hot to drink and hearty to eat. We sat down, looked at the map, and saw that we would have to ride north back through the full stretch of the Black Hills.

Riding through the hills had been incredible going south, so we figured the trip back north would not be disappointing. Even with the delays from the rain and construction, there was plenty of time left in the day. And if needed, we knew we could skip out on going to Devil's Tower if our (my) mood was too sour and just head to the hotel.

The nice thing about the ride back north was that we did not need to travel on any of the same roads we had chosen to ride southbound on. The roads of the Black Hills were all figure eights that interwove like a double helix intersecting back to each other every so often. We rode different DNA strands all the way back up to Lead City, and took another pit stop to fill up with gas and have more hot fluids pumped into our frigid bodies. It wasn't that cold outside, but being wet on a cloudy day and riding at speed can become fairly uncomfortable.

I had made a poor choice in gloves. They no longer provided me with warmth and just kept my hands constantly soaked. But without them the wind chill seemed to have even more of a negative effect.

I was mentally chalking up the gloves and rain gear as miserable failures that were not to be used for any future expeditions. Unfortunately, there was no changing them out now, as this was just the first day on the bike out of sixteen. All I could do was hope that it wouldn't rain the entire time.

We got back on the road to Route 90 and gunned it for the Wyoming border. It was still unclear at that time if we had the desire, time, or motivation to see Devil's Tower. Yet there was hope in our souls as we looked westward and saw blue skies.

As soon as we passed the "Welcome to Wyoming" sign, the sun proudly burst through the clouds, truly welcoming us into the Cowboy State. It was amazing to know that the sun's rays of light, coming from ninety-three million miles away, and taking around eight minutes and twenty seconds to get to earth, were finally able to hit us instead of some cloud hovering just above where we rode.

We pulled into the visitor center a few miles across the border to breathe in the new state's air and collect ourselves.

I gathered some pamphlets about Devil's Tower while I spoke to a woman about the weather forecast. She pointed to a live feed from the tower on one of the display screens and things looked to be sunny. It seemed like our luck was changing.

She then marked on a map a less-traveled back entrance road that she highly recommended for unique vantage points. We took the map, along with our rejuvenated spirits, and followed the advice of the kind and informative lady.

States shouldn't have such a clear and cut division of landscape, especially ones that are in the shape of squares, but once we entered Wyoming, we could just feel we were in another state. The vegetation, colors, and land formations were so uniquely different from South Dakota that we needed no "Welcome to Wyoming" sign to know we had entered a different portion of the country.

Riding along, we caught sight of hills that seemed to rise out of the landscape like whales cresting out of the water. The colorful splashes of rock layers looked as if it was an imitation of a child's watercolor picture, but it was real, and it was astonishing.

Our eyes searched around every bend for what could be Devil's Tower but once we saw it, there was no mistaking it for any other landmark.

Because I could not judge our distance from the tower, it was unclear just how immense the butte really was. With every passing mile, the huge growth emerging from the earth was far larger than I had imagined, even when we were fully anticipating to see such a large structure rising out of the ground.

The view from afar was wonderful, but we wanted to pull in and take a better look at the goliath. I had purchased a National Park Pass prior to our trip knowing that we would be visiting seven or so National Parks (Mount Rushmore's parking lot is not a National Park).

As we pulled up to the little toll booth to show the park pass, the tower seemed to grow a foot every inch we rode forward. It was only when we parked at the base that we fully understood its enormity.

Riding in open air with the sun finally shining on us had air-dried the outer shells of our rain suits, and I wanted to rid myself of mine fully. So I stripped off my gear and draped it across the KTM to dry.

Taking off the rain gear was a pain in the ass. I had to first take off my little boot covers that Velcroed and zipped up the side of my boot, then take off my boots to remove my rain pants, but I was glad to discard them for the day. Marisa, on the other hand, did not take off her raingear, knowing if it rained again, she'd have to put it all back on.

There was a trail that led around the base of the tower. Kids of all ages climbed up the large rocks that had fallen and tumbled to the ground over the centuries of erosion. We opted for a couple of photos and sat on a bench to let the sun suck the remaining precipitation out of our clothing.

It had been a long day. A long, wet day full of spectacular sights, and the road's peaks and valleys seemed to match some of our emotional highs and lows. All leading us to where we sat now, absorbing in the day as the sun absorbed the moisture out.

We were about an hour from the hotel in Gillette and estimated there was an hour or so left of sunlight. So I stuffed my rain gear into the T-Bag, threw on my leather jacket, and we proceeded south towards I-90 West.

After three minutes on the road it began to drizzle. I had to pull over and remove all the rain gear that I had so arrogantly put away a few minutes before. Frustrated with my defeat at the hands of mother nature, I donned my suit of elementally weak armor, and we continued into Gillette in the rain. A short time later we arrived at the last hotel bed we would be sleeping in for the next four days.

Because the KTM had a chain drive, I periodically had to clean and lube the chain, especially during really wet conditions, or if any extended off-road riding took place. After the day we had just endured, I knew it was time to clean it.

I had spotted one of those do-it-yourself car washes with a spray nozzle on the way into town, so I rode my bike over to give her a shower after dropping Marisa off at the hotel.

As I pulled in and set the bike on the center stand, a car pulled up in front of the stall, and a shady-looking man covered in tattoos stepped out.

"Hey, man," he said to me, walking over. "We gotta to stick together, you know," he rambled, pounding his chest with a closed palm.

"Damn straight," I said nervously, figuring I should just agree with him.

"It's a brotherhood man. We're havin' a meeting at the bowling alley on Third and Main at midnight. You should meet us there," he formally invited me.

"Yes, sir, I will try to make it if I can," I replied as I put the last quarter in the machine, activating the apparatus.

Our conversation was thankfully interrupted by the loud humming of the pressure washer. I gave him a thumbs up, turned my back, and started cleaning my bike.

I was very nervous about the whole encounter, and I figured it was best to appease his mindless rants, but now I just wanted him to leave.

As he finally got back in his car, he yelled over the noise, "Good luck, brother! I hope to see you tonight!"

By the grace of God, he drove away without questioning my commitment to the brotherhood or quizzing me on any details regarding the issue.

Completely dumbstruck, I looked down at my clothes, trying to figure out why this guy thought that I (not a very intimidating-looking person) or my adventure motorcycle (not a mean-looking chopper) had any affiliation with gang activity.

Then I noticed I was wearing my red neck warmer/headband, multi-use tube thingamajigger, and just to be clear, it was not intended to be a gang-related red colored neck warmer/headband multi-use tube thingamajigger. It was worn purely out of fashion as it did very little for wind protection or as a water repellent, but it did look cool. I could only assume he thought I was a Blood?

I took it off immediately and stuffed it in my pocket. I was happy I was not wearing Marisa's blue one as the whole incident could have gone down far worse.

I washed my bike as quickly as I could, cleaned and lubed the chain, then rode back to the hotel and the safety of our room. I told Marisa the story, and we both laughed it off, but it was not as funny in the moment.

Breaking the promise I made to the nice man, I went to sleep with no intentions of bowling, or of wearing anything red the next day.

Chapter 5 - A Good Sign

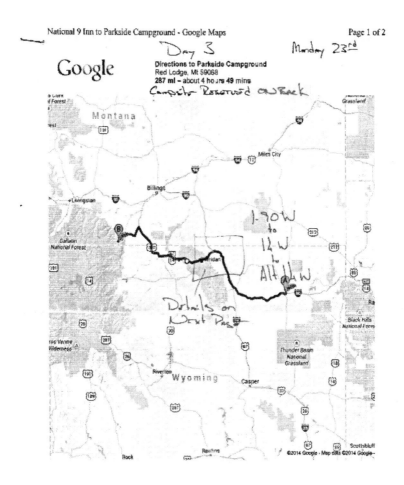

National 9 Inn to Parkside Campground - Google Maps   Page 1 of 2

Google

Day 3   Monday 23rd

Directions to Parkside Campground
Red Lodge, Mt 59068
287 ml – about 4 hours 49 mins

Campsite Reserved on Back

1.90W
to
1½ W
to
Alt ¼ W

Details on
Next Page

We woke up to grey skies above. The weather app on my phone confirmed a full day's worth of possible showers. The plan was to ride a total of 290 miles in just under five hours, and it looked like it was going to rain the entire time.

The Google Maps I had printed at home prior to the trip represented an overall average of the day. Logged on to a computer back in Illinois while lying in bed, these maps provided an itinerary in which I could drag and change our route off the major highways and reroute us through clusters of forests and backroads leading in the same general direction.

What these maps could not predict were all the side roads we kept turning onto to explore, nor did they represent the time we took to stare at the wonders of nature we came upon. And of course, they did not take into account delays due to inclement weather. They were a good best-case scenario if we were to program the bike to ride on autopilot through a vacuum of space, refusing to appreciate our surroundings.

The original estimate quickly turned into 340 miles in seven hours by the end of the day without much effort.

For the second day in a row we got into our ever-so-stylish, comfortable, and totally breathable rain gear. There was nothing more satisfying than putting on a garbage bag as a T-shirt in the morning.

We loaded the panniers back onto the bike and headed west. After an hour of riding on the highway in light rain, we arrived in Sheridan, Wyoming. We needed to stop at an electronics store because the memory cards we had been using for our camera and GoPro knockoff were filling up much faster than we had anticipated.

While we stood in the parking lot of the store, we looked at the Bighorn Mountains that ascended from the landscape ahead of us. We had been riding in the rain all morning, but what lurked in and above those mountain ranges looked like a good place to build a replica of Count Dracula's castle.

Dark clouds engulfed the peaks, and foggy mist crawled down its sides. Nothing about the range was inviting but was instead a visual equivalent to a rattlesnake's distinctive alert, warning us not to come any closer, unless we were up for a fight.

Marisa and I discussed staying on I-90 as it would avoid the Bighorns and reroute us to Billings, Montana, but that would slightly redirect us out of our way. But I wanted a third opinion.

I spoke to a couple of locals in the store to feel out their thoughts. I really wanted to ride through the mountains, but there were confirmations that it had been snowing along the mountain pass the day before, conditions that could have left the sharp cutbacks going back and forth up the mountainside covered in ice and snow.

I was upset at the thought of missing the Bighorns because this was one of the childhood memories that I wanted to relive as an adult. My father took my family through this same pass twenty years prior, and this flashback of my youth was like recapturing a fragment of a dream. I couldn't recall any detail, but I was left with a warm fuzzy feeling when I reflected on it. Plus, the Bighorns were that day's only point of interest, and if skipped, we would spend the day accumulating nothing but highway miles.

On the other hand, riding through icy mountain roads while wearing a garbage bag didn't have the same charm as my childhood memories provided.

Being stubborn, I decided that not only might we never get the chance to ride through them again, but I also did not want to be driven away from a primary waypoint because of less-than-ideal weather conditions.

Marisa, who as before mentioned hates the rain and cold, just smiled and said, "Let's do it," knowing we were about to ride into the heart of a storm at elevation.

With the addition of a long-sleeve shirt under my fancy garbage bag and rain gear, we rode into the Bighorns, accepting the challenges of what might lie beyond the pass.

It was quite chilling riding into that dark accumulation of clouds. Excitement was mixed with apprehension, knowing it very well could turn out to be an unpleasant experience, all based on my uncompromising relentlessness. As we began the switchbacks making our way up the side of the ridges, I started to doubt my decision.

We were the only vehicle on the road. This hinted the locals knew that today was a good day to take the long way around. However, being the only commuter let me adopt the speed I felt most comfortable riding at with no pressure from behind.

The rain started to come down heavily, but the tires stuck solidly to the road. As we continued to gain in altitude, the banks of the road turned to snow. This was the first snow sighting of the trip, and it was pretty mesmerizing to see snow in late June. The snowbanks on the side of the road stretched farther outward into the landscape the more we climbed skyward.

Once we reached the top of the pass, we realized the mountains were what seemed to be the birthplace of the miserable weather, for just beyond the grip of the peaks lay clear blue skies.

Our view to the horizon was split in half. Dreary clouds hung intimidatingly above, while a pristine and immaculate blue was painted on the lower portion of our visual canvas. It was a direct representation of heaven and hell but flipped upside down.

With new vigor, we continued down the other side. Sharp switchbacks led us into a land of unaccustomed sunshine and warmth.

At the bottom of the pass, we pulled off the road to look back at what we had just accomplished. (44.797681, -107.987240) We took a couple of photos of the two of us with the bike and the Bighorns behind us

Those pictures turned out to be some of my favorite, partially due to an ordinary road sign with an arrow pointing to the right. The sign had turned the same colors as the mountainous background from years of slight rusting. Yellows, reds, oranges, and deep blacks were represented in the old sign as well as the ancient mountain's ridges. Both affected by the same symptoms of nature's wrath and erosion.

I don't know why I liked that sign so much, but Marisa was hungry, so I had to part ways with it. I took its advice and turned right as one last tribute to our encounter. It was a good sign.

A few short miles later, I pulled over once again. With the sun fully out and clear skies ahead of us, I repacked my rain gear after my disrobing ritual, and threw on my leather jacket. Marisa refused to remove her rain gear once again; to her it was worth the inconvenience of bearing the extra material than any chance of rain hitting her exposed clothing.

The problem for me was that the plastic bag I had to wear, along with the synthetic plastic material that made up the fabric of the pants and jacket, did not breathe. This trapped any heat my body produced inside my own personal greenhouse, effectively turning the ensemble into a sweat suit.

I couldn't understand how Marisa could deal with the buildup of heat while in the direct sun. My best guess was that she was a cold-blooded creature, and she needed to retain as much body heat as possible to maintain the same temperature that my body naturally sustained in normal conditions. That was the only explanation that made sense to me.

As we rode the remaining distance to Red Lodge, Montana, the weather seemed to be holding out, and it was turning into an enjoyable ride.

A large contributing factor in making the ride more pleasant for these longer stretches of road was a helmet-to-helmet wired intercom system Marisa and I had. The one we purchased was twelve dollars. It was a plastic, directly-wired, and battery-powered system we purchased online, and it did exactly what was needed most of the time, and nothing more. It was complete garbage above fifty miles an hour because of wind interference, but we both wore three-quarter face helmets, so I do not believe the two-hundred-dollar-plus mics would have fared any better.

"An ou ehr me?" Marisa would shout into the microphone.

"What?"

"Can ou ear knee?" She would repeat even louder, but still just as unclear.

"Sure," I would reply half the time just to keep the conversation flowing.

"I ave to oh to the math room illy rilly add," she would scream loud enough for me to hear through the back of my helmet with no speaker system necessary.

"Okay, sounds good."

"Ank ou," she ended the fuzzy transmission.

We quickly adapted to using hand signals for some of the more primitive functions of the human body.

The intercom was more useful along the slow, twisting roads where four eyes were better than two in spotting unique natural formations or wildlife. I strongly recommend a microphone system for any two-up riders out there, but I also suggest spending more than twelve dollars on a set.

As we entered Red Lodge, Montana, a quaint town with little tourist shops, all we had to work with was a GPS coordinate of 45° 3' 43" N and 109° 24' 32" W for the campground where we had our reservation. This turned out to be quite a difficult place to reach because our GPS was not functioning in this semi-remote location.

The map I printed was an eagle-eye view of the area, but we knew the campground should have been between Red Lodge and Beartooth Pass (the road leading over the neighboring mountains), and so if we reached Beartooth Pass, we had gone too far.

After a few miles, we reached the looming mountains ahead of us with signs reading "Beartooth Pass," so we turned around to scout the area going back in the other direction. Then we hit Red Lodge again with no successful sightings of the campground, which meant we must have passed it twice.

I pulled over to the side of the road and tried to call the campground, only to reach a voicemail stating it was an unmanned campground and to enjoy our stay. Frustrated, we rode down the same road looking for the Parkside Campground sign until we hit the entrance to Beartooth Pass for the second time. It seemed road gremlins were on the loose and hiding any signage for our destination.

To literally dampen my mood further, it began to rain. I pulled over and put on my rain gear in defeat, Marisa was conveniently already in hers.

Marisa spotted a forest ranger building and hoped that they might be able to assist two lost souls, but the ranger station was closed. It was around five o'clock on a Monday and irritation was beginning to consume me.

We headed back down in the direction of Beartooth for one more run before my patience was going to expire and we would just have to ride to the nearest hotel back in Red Lodge.

The campground ended up being much farther southwest than I had judged on the map, and it turned out the only gremlin on the road was me.

We finally pulled in to find an elegant and truly hidden treasure. There was a river running through the middle of the campground, and we found our site with a grand view of the bluffs directly across from the roaring river. The rain, that seemed to have been coming down since the dawn of time, had elevated the water to the highest edge of the bank.

Marisa and I quickly set up our tent and headed inside to change into our now diminishing supply of dry clothing. We were both hungry, so I figured I would brave the rain and cook us up some food using our little portable stove and some dehydrated food bags.

At home, I am known to friends and family to be good at adding the final touches to dishes, putting in spices and herbs to enhance the flavor of an existing dish. I do not fare well with the origins or the creation of the dish itself. I am an improver of food and should never be left alone in the production of food, pre-packaged or not.

What I served that night was gruel at best. The noodles were hard, whatever flavor I had chosen was lost in the abundance of lukewarm water as the flavored powder had all settled to the bottom in clumps. But the need for substance was overwhelming, and we tried to eat the abomination I had created.

The rain settled down to a slow rhythm on the rainfly of the tent. We peeked outside to take another look at our surroundings and found we had neighbors. A man and his family were in an RV two spots down from us. He walked over and introduced himself as Matt.

"So, you folks are from Illinois?" he asked, pronouncing the "s" in Illinois. "Judging by your plate there on your motorcycle."

"Yes, sir, long ride from home, but only the second day on the bike," I said as I introduced Marisa and myself.

"You and your wife hungry? We just grilled up some burgers about an hour ago."

"Yes, we are, the food Tim made is absolutely horrific," Marisa said almost before Matt finished his invitation.

"She's not my wife, were just dating as of now," I said at the same time Marisa understated how awesome my cooking was.

Marisa and I gave each other a cold stare.

"Well come on over, we've got plenty of dry wood, food, and beer."

We most graciously accepted his invitation. With a cooler of beer popped open, we spent hours sharing jokes, local history (since Matt was from the area), good food, and spirits.

Matt informed us that Beartooth Pass would be a much greater task to traverse than the Bighorns. "The elevation is a lot higher than the Bighorns," he explained. "They just opened the road to Beartooth for the first time this season two days ago. Before that, it was closed due to the snow."

"We'll be alright," I said confidently.

"Beartooth ain't no joke, man," he warned. "And I hope you have more than that thin shirt and a garbage bag to keep you warm up there."

"It is friggin' June, I didn't bring any winter gear." I told him of the clothes I had, and what I planned to wear while going over the pass. Which was essentially a shirt, a garbage bag, and a leather jacket.

"Go back to Red Lodge and get yourself something you won't freeze in," he recommended.

"We're going back to Red Lodge then," Marisa stated as a fact.

Even though I felt like I had ridden to Red Lodge ten times throughout the day, I figured it was best to listen to the local when it came to a subject he knew much more about than I.

After our share of conversation, food, and drinks, we said goodnight to our hospitable neighbors and headed back to our tent for a good night's sleep. The next morning, we would once again backtrack into town, eat some breakfast, purchase a heavy sweater or two, and be on with our day.

We drifted into sleep to the sounds of a rushing river, the crackling of our neighbor's dying embers, and hundreds of different hoots of bird calls, insects, and mammals all working together in the symphony of nature.

Chapter 6 - Bear Teeth and Buffalo

I think I could begin every chapter with "we woke up to grey skies above." However, there was a method to my madness of planning the trip from late June into early July.

I realized there would always be the chance of rain during those months, though I would have never guessed this daily onslaught. But the rain brought new life to the scenery. The greens became greener, the contrast against the arid landscape made all of the other colors tucked away in the bluffs pop out more vibrantly. Flamboyant flowers bloomed in deep pink, red, and yellow clusters on the sides of the road, as if they had just blossomed the day before.

I remembered from my family's road trip that the Badlands were a dead and barren place. My memories recall only slightly different tones of brown, but because of all the current precipitation when Marisa and I went, the landscape had been resurrected into an existence of pure beauty. The ranger in the Badlands had warned us that the vibrant colors would fade to the browns of dead foliage in the next couple weeks with the upcoming heat.

Also, leaving slightly earlier allowed us the comfort of knowing that while camping throughout Utah's deserts, we wouldn't suffer heat stroke from the extremely high temperatures in July and August. The cold was uncomfortable, but intense heat just drained the life force and energy out of me.

Even with all that in mind, as I crawled out of our tent I swore out loud. Another round of aggressive, low-hanging clouds dangled above us.

"Marisa, looks like another day of getting soaked to the bone," I stated as I boiled water to get some instant coffee in me (the sweet nectar of life), and so that Marisa could make her morning tea.

Marisa mumbled something unintelligible through the walls of the tent.

During our breakfast of oatmeal and our hot drink of choice, I summoned the day's agenda from our luggage like an envelope containing the surprising next step from *The Amazing Race*. The packets of daily information were kept in chronological order in a large plastic freezer bag.

The day's ride seemed easy enough compared to the previous combination of weather and our quest to find the campground. So we packed the panniers, rolled up the tent, loaded the bike, and headed into Red Lodge for what was hopefully the last time on the trip.

After the purchase of a new, extra-warm, and way-too-expensive zip-up hoodie for myself, we put on our tried and not-so-true rain gear and headed back to Beartooth Pass.

The frustrations of the last few days melted away within the first few minutes of ascending the pass. Midwesterners such as ourselves rarely get to see sights like these, and there was a lot to take in.

Immense granite peaks jutted out of the plateau, surrounding us on all sides as we followed the single road through the giants. They looked down in judgement from their high stature as we progressed along the small, winding path cut into their side. Like watching ants preforming their daily tasks under the kitchen sink, they must have wondered, "What the hell are they doing here?"

As a child, on these same roads in the back of a station wagon, I remembered there not being any side rails, something I kept tormenting Marisa about leading up to the pass. My father would ride all the way onto the shoulder, well past the white line marking the safe zone that sane fathers should abide by, only to get the desired reaction of complete and total fear from his innocent children.

I very much wanted to pass this tradition on to Marisa, but to my dismay, they had erected guard rails. Too many fathers like mine had played this game, and the state was forced to issue laws against the torture of small children. The bill was most likely voted into effect by all of the wives of the husbands who took part in this cruel act.

The switchbacks were broken up by short sections of straightaways, only to turn back again and elevate farther up the mountainside. As we rose higher and higher, the views became increasingly grand.

The snow banks of the Bighorns we experienced the day before were nothing compared to the ten-foot drifts on either side of this road. The views of the snow-capped mountains in the distance were breathtaking. Jaw-dropping ridges plunged thousands of feet straight down and disappeared into the jagged landscape.

Marisa's trigger finger was getting a full workout while taking rapid-fire pictures of our surroundings. The sun even peeked out, piercing the clouds with its light-ray fingers as if to take a look at the majestic landscape below. Of course, it quickly disappeared once it saw that I noticed it.

We reached a pull-off at the very edge of a ridge, dismounted, and surrounded by stillness, took in the view. To our surprise, even with gusts of wind, it was not uncomfortably cold. I had zero memory of this impressive vista from my childhood. There were no hints in the furthest reaches of my mind that recalled ever seeing what lay before us. A straight row of mountains divided the landscape, the peaks of each individual mountain a perfect replica of the Rockies as a whole.

The clouds just above and in the distance were dark swabs of cotton made of the same tones and colors of the scenery below. It was as if an artist had used the same palette of oils to paint the distant mountains, clouds, and sky. The road was the only exception not made from the same pigments, but I was happy it was there.

A fellow biker had stopped in the pull-off and graciously took a couple of pictures of us with our camera. We shared short stories of what was ahead and behind us on our journey. The rider said we were near the top of the pass, so we parted ways and pressed forward to see what wonders lay on the other side.

The road's graceful sweeping descent allowed for long and tight leaning of the motorcycle. Riding at my own pace without butting up to the vehicle in front of me, or causing delays to anyone behind, I settled into the flow of the turns. I would not say I was no longer paying attention, but my mind was clear as I floated in slow motion along the twisting roads.

Suddenly, I was snapped out of this tranquil moment of inner peace as suicidal crotch rocketeers zipped by in a race for death. I wanted no part of their antics and pulled onto the right shoulder to slow down.

I have never supported a cruiser versus crotch rocket mentality. Nor stated that one is better than the other or prejudged anyone because of the bike they chose to ride, but the stupid things you see people do on motorcycles mostly seems to happen only on the latter of the two. I do not want to call out the entire family of sport bike riders, idiots are plentiful across the board, but at the time I was cursing this particular group as they roared past.

I think George Carlin said it best, and I completely agree that, "Anyone going slower than you is an ass, and anyone going faster than you is a lunatic." Don't get me wrong, I've leaned into hairpin turns as fast as I possibly could. I still haven't fully outgrown those thrill-seeking moments, but I do recognize the appropriate times to do so, when any acts of complete stupidity would only cause bodily harm to myself.

The seven bikes that zoomed by me going seventy miles an hour while I was doing thirty-five, was only the first of many heats in the Russian roulette race to come. Instead of the scenery, I was now focused on not getting killed by one of these maniacs and was much tenser than just seconds before.

Marisa kept a watchful eye behind us and let me know when the next round of fools emerged from the bend so I could pull over not to be bothered by these demons of speed. After five more minutes of defensive riding, the groups of crazies had finally all passed and we could sink back into the inner subconscious of our peaceful voyage down the road.

At the bottom of the mountain pass there was a half-frozen lake that perfectly mirrored the sky above. Pure white snow lay on patches of ice, and melting ice gave off a blue hue all framed by a mountainous landscape in the distance. (44.940748, -109.506183)

The elaborate colors and landscape seemed to be the finalized painting out of an episode of *The Joy of Painting* with Bob Ross. I could hear him in the back of my head, "Now here lives a crooked little tree, maybe he's a politician," as he brushed on a perfect little bent tree in just a few strokes.

As we gazed back at the road we had travelled, feeling a sense of pride about our latest achievement, a single Harley with a couple riding two-up pulled into our exclusively romantic lake. We exchanged greetings and cameras with the husband and wife duo to take pictures, even though you wouldn't know it was Marisa in the picture with me.

I was starting to call Marisa "Marvin the Martian" because the entire trip she would never take the time to remove her helmet for any of the pictures because of the trouble it took to do so. In every photo she was this tiny frame with a big bobble-head.

After taking pictures with the exquisite backdrop, the couple asked us what lay ahead since they were traveling in the opposite direction.

"The only inconveniences are not of nature, but of man and his relentless need for speed and adrenaline," I spat out harshly due to the recent frustrations.

"The ride was beautiful," Marisa chimed in, lowering the threat level back down to reality. "You will enjoy every second of it."

The wife nodded. "So where're you guys headed?"

"We're on our way to Yellowstone to camp for the next three nights," I informed them.

"Hopefully it's stopped snowing," the man stated nonchalantly.

I whispered under my breath, "Snowing?"

Marisa shot me a concerned glance.

I have been known to underprepare in certain instances. I have flown to Key West without a swimsuit or sunglasses. But in this case, it was a shock that on June 24th there was a chance of snow near a geothermal active super-volcano. The fact that Yellowstone is at an average of eight thousand feet above sea level had not occurred to me. Another lesson learned while on my first go-around on a motorcycle: prepare for every type of weather.

With a snowy campground to look forward to for the next three nights, we moved ahead. Around twenty miles beyond the pass we pulled into an attractive little mountain town. We refueled the bike and needed a little refueling ourselves. So we found ourselves at a small bistro and ordered some hot soup to chase away the chill.

There was a market built up of small tents across the street selling trinkets and souvenirs to tourists, so I walked over to see if anything caught my eye. There were T-shirts, bumper stickers, and a whole slew of odds and ends desperately trying to grab a buyer's attention. On a table were knives of all fashions, from huge Davy Crockett knives and machetes, all the way down to little pocketknives.

One of the pocketknives had an engraving of two wolves howling under a full moon. I thought Marisa would enjoy it, and might turn out to be quite useful along our trip. Souvenirs are hard to bring along on a motorcycle, as every square inch of space is needed. But this pocketknife fit the carry-on luggage qualifications of the pannier's available space, and I bought it for fifteen dollars. I walked back across the street and presented the gift to Marisa, who, as expected, loved it.

"It's perfect!" she said with big doe eyes and a beaming smile.

Rarely have I been able to successfully attain that exact reaction out of her when hoped for. The proof that it is the small things in life was represented by the look in her eyes.

"The wolves are like us under the stars," she said, then leaned in and kissed me as a reward for my efforts.

We finished our meal and prepared to re-board our mode of transportation. I wanted to get to Yellowstone while the sun was still out so we could begin looking at the wide variety of attractions. We would be camping there for the next three nights, but with Yellowstone being so grand, spreading across thirty-five hundred square miles, I wanted to jump-start getting as many of the landmarks and sightseeing in as we could.

Technically, we were already in Yellowstone National Park, but I wanted to reach the central hub where the main attractions were all located. Our campground was the southernmost camp in the park, about four hours away. I planned this so we could depart on the third day without having to ride through the entire park to continue on south to the Grand Tetons and beyond.

The majority of the thirty-five hundred square miles of the national park is back-country. Those sections are truly remote areas that the common tourist will never see. Anyone who plans on camping and hiking into the wild back-country of Yellowstone must have a permit, sign waivers, be in top physical form, be riddled with bells to ward off bears, and carry bear mace if the bear-repelling bells do not work as intended.

As much as we would have loved to, we would not be experiencing those sections of the park. We would be sticking to the more family-oriented sections, where wildlife and natural formations were still abundant, but with no chance of our journey turning out like *Into the Wild*.

Marisa and I rode west on 212 and got to the junction we needed to turn south onto Grand Loop Road. We once again rode through valleys surrounded by monstrous mountain ranges. There was a heavy overcast sky above, but we had grown accustomed to the constant presence of the grey vault.

Finally, we noticed real-life buffalo grazing in the not too distant green valleys. We saw their dark silhouettes spread across the landscape like poppy seeds on a hamburger bun, so we pulled over to look at the newest marvel of the journey.

It turned out that buffalo were everywhere in Yellowstone. Marisa was shooting pictures of a group to the left, then a hundred more on the right, and only a few miles later another two hundred freely roamed across a wide valley with a small, twisting river running through it. The farther we drove into the park, the more frequently buffalo appeared, as well as the number of cars that built up as families stopped to stare at the majestic beasts.

This time, the bison were truly free-roaming, and when they wished to travel from here to there and a road lay between the two points, they simply walked across. Cars stopped and people watched with wonder as a herd of fifty bison would walk lazily across the road. Baby bison running hurriedly next to their mothers induced "oohs" and "ahhhs" from the line of patiently waiting onlookers.

Some people would open their doors and walk out of their cars for better photos, only to scurry back into the car at the slightest movement from the beasts in their direction. There were plenty of postings stating not to feed or approach the wildlife because they were in every sense of the word wild and very unpredictable.

We were about the fifth vehicle in the procession of cars behind a group of crossing bison. Granted, we were getting excellent pictures, but it was kind of nerve-wracking. I turned off the bike's engine to avoid startling any of the creatures. This now meant we were completely exposed without the safety of windows or doors, on a vehicle that was not even running.

I kept telling Marisa (as well as myself) that the risk was low, but I had no idea what would happen if one of those beasts got pissy, or what it even took to make one pissy, but I was not going to contribute anything that could lead to one indeed getting pissy.

Once the parade of bison had passed, we carried on into the park. But the number of times people just stopped in the middle of the road to stare into the distance at objects just out of sight was far too often. We were riding down two-lane roads, one lane each direction, with no real shoulder but plenty of pull-offs on either side of the road, which people were not using.

Yellowstone was a new type of beauty to everyone, including us, and it was understandable why people were stopping to stare out into the distance, but this was causing a constant backup of traffic. The momentary delays were not too frustrating at first, but three cars ahead was a family that would stop to look at geese on the side of the road, and then stop to look at buffalo two miles into the hills. They were not using the pull-offs to let us pass, and in my opinion, stopping for less-than-satisfactory reasons.

Around the fifth time we came to a complete stop for seemingly nothing, I figured I would overtake this car of casual sightseeing folk.

I was only going ten miles an hour around the three cars in front of me when a buffalo almost T-boned me from the right. As it turned out, the sightseeing "boy who cried wolf" lead car, actually saw a buffalo just as I chose to be rid of their pestering slowness. The universe had pulled a bait-and-switch on me. I was sure a divine being was giggling somewhere in the cosmos from the look on my face.

"You got me that time," I whispered, both thanking and cursing the same deity for the narrow miss.

I couldn't believe I was almost the jackass on the six o'clock news who got hit by a buffalo crossing the road. From that point on, I would be coming to a complete stop and patiently waiting until the flow of traffic continued.

I felt like an ass and wanted to get well in front of the cars that had just witnessed the stupidity I displayed. Marisa was not so happy with my decision-making skills either. She promised not to tell anyone that I almost got us both hit by a bison if I promised to ride more safely.

As we entered the main touristy part of the park, we immediately found ourselves at a pull-off overlooking the Yellowstone River. It was very clear to see how the park got its name, if there was any confusion to begin with. The bluffs of the canyon opposite us were made up of yellows, tans, and oranges freckled with bright green trees hanging on for dear life, sinking their roots into the rocky earth like hooks. The river cutting its way through the canyon below was the same clear blue that comes to mind when picturing the Caribbean Ocean.

I could only imagine that vantage points like this one would become just as frequent as the buffalo. Everything was so unbelievable, I could not digest that we were actually in Yellowstone riding around in the open air while peacefully relaxed on the KTM.

Marisa and I worked our way south through the park in the direction of our campground. With plenty of daylight left, we took the time to pull over whenever we saw a sign for natural hot springs, geysers, or other geothermal pools.

As we pulled into one of the lots, we noticed the asphalt of the parking lot had sections that the forces of nature were taking back as its own. Holes appeared in the paved surface where the tarmac sunk back into the earth, the smell of sulfur and the gurgling of boiling water coming from just below.

I found them fascinating, but the little holes in the parking lot turned out not to be the most impressive sights around. Marisa had already moved on to the enormous thermal pools beyond the stone barrier.

Draped by mountains in the far background, a large valley covered in green grass spread out before us, leading up to a forest. Abruptly, the trees cleared into a small patch of barren and dead land containing the pools. The sulfur and heat were killing the grasses and poisoning the trees surrounding the area. There was a lonely buffalo on the side of one of the pools, completing the memorable snapshot in my mind.

As we pushed southward, there were countless places for us to stop and just stare for hours every turn in the road. Rivers cutting through the green valleys of rolling slopes. Lumbering buffalo, that I now had a new-found respect for, roamed those same hills. The sun faded in and out as overcast clouds chased each other across the sky, with each changing tone of light a new version of the sublime landscape was presented before us.

We took our time, but remained aware that we needed to get to the campground to set up our home base for the next three nights, so we moved in the direction of our temporary residence.

There were no dull or boring moments during the ride to our camp. On our right were forests filled with creatures as exotic to me as if I were on the Galapagos Islands. We already had sightings of elk, deer, and coyotes. We really wanted to see a bear or a moose, but were more than satisfied with the wildlife list we had checked off so far.

On the left side of our regal voyage was the glimmering of Lake Yellowstone, with snow-peaked mountains on its far side. A thin wall of trees standing tall and proud like British Royal Guards in single formation rose between the road and the lake. Their random spacing turned into an emotional game of peek-a-boo as we were teased with views of the captivating lake, only to have them disappear again until the next gap.

Grant Village is one of eight tiny little towns throughout the park. Only five of those eight towns have all the amenities within a short distance, including a general store, gas station, showers, and a laundromat. These five locations are usually the first to be filled due to their proximity to modern conveniences. Knowing this, I had booked our reservations online six months prior, knowing that Yellowstone became full very quickly in the prime of tourist season.

I had requested a large site, figuring it would be nice to have more room between us and our neighbors. I had to list the length and quantity of vehicles there would be on site, so I was forced to confirm that I only had one motorcycle, which is kind of contradictory for a large site. But I hoped for the best.

We pulled into Grant Village's check-in cabin, parked the motorcycle, and stripped off the layers of clothes we had on, including my non-breathable rain tuxedo that was neither rainproof nor fashionable, but was now worn purely out of habit. We walked up to the cabin's window prepared with the reservation that I had printed out.

I showed our booking receipt where a large site had been requested on a first-come, first-serve basis to the lady behind the counter. I explained that we had indeed arrived, and would be staying with a motorcycle, but just wanted a little extra plush room between us and the next campsite if available. Or at best, we wanted a tent-only loop of the campground so we would not be stuck in the middle of an RV metropolis. We also did not want to be right next to the bathrooms because of the high volume of traffic during all hours of the day, as well as throughout the night.

The lady behind the counter said she would do what she could to best suit our requests.

I had put a deposit down for the reservation on the website, and that deposit should have been deducted from the total charge once paid in full. The lovely lady who was assisting us was a new recruit to the campground, and she did not understand the notion that I had already paid for the first night and now only owed for the remaining two. I displayed the online receipt proving the portion of the payment already paid, with the total remaining listed below.

This clearly was a new world filled with strange concepts and math skills that our host did not understand. A supervisor had to be called into the office, my card needed to be credited the full amount instead of just a third for some reason, then charged for the two nights by themselves. We walked away with four receipts of various charges and credits, just happy we could finally set up camp and get something to eat.

Marisa and I looked at the campground map and found our site easily. It was in the middle of a steep hill, had two trees defining the boundaries between our site, and the sites on either side of us which were occupied by giant recreational vehicles only about fifteen feet away. Across the tiny road was another huge humming RV, and directly behind us: the bathroom. I was less than pleased, to say the least.

Disheartened as I was, there was no way I was going to ride back up to the office and complain. Such is life, and I figured maybe this was the park's spirit getting back at me for almost hitting an innocent buffalo. Campground karma at its best.

Parking the bike was a pain because of the steep incline, but I left it in gear to lock the wheels and began to unpack everything. We wanted to set up the tent the furthest away from both the bathroom and the road.

What would have been the best location was taken up by a trench that ran through the campsite that we could only assume was the path water took when it rained. And one thing we knew for sure was that at any given second, there was a possible chance of rain. The good news was that the likelihood of snow was now near zero percent. Although it was cold, it would most likely not drop below freezing in the next few days.

Due to the limited selection of good spots, we set the tent up in the far corner of the plot of rented land, nearest to the bathrooms, but away from any watery canals that would lead directly to our front door if it rained hard enough.

With our temporary home set up in the best position we could, we headed out to dinner at a fancy restaurant that we passed on the way in. It was close enough not to throw on our helmets, but we did keep our rain suits handy.

We are not usually fancy restaurant folk, but it was either that or go to the general store to buy beans and hot dogs to cook up on a fire. I figured an amazing day should be followed by an amazing meal, so we rode the bike to the restaurant just outside of the campground.

The restaurant sat on a bluff above Yellowstone Lake with spectacular views that reached out into the distance. We requested a table for two and were told that there was an hour wait, but we could sit at the bar until a table was open.

Not wanting to wait an hour, nor in the mood to drink, I asked if there was anywhere else in close proximity for dining. The host confirmed there was another restaurant just down the path that sat at the base of the lake.

It began to pour as soon as we walked outside. We figured we might as well gun it for the restaurant at the bottom of the hill on foot.

We jogged the quarter mile to the other restaurant and burst through the double doors completely soaked even though we had our rain gear on. We did not have our helmets, so water just flowed down our necks into all the little nooks and crannies of our suits.

As we shed our wet outer layers, Marisa and I picked a booth in front of the large windows.

The restaurant was built over the lake so our view was similar to being at the end of a pier with a most intimate and magnificent perspective. As we sat down, our server came by and introduced himself as Phil. Our strange, wet uniforms laying on the booth led to questions about our mode of transportation and led to short stories of where we came from and where we were going.

We learned Phil had recently graduated from high school and had lived his entire life in Minnesota. After graduation, he decided to take a year off to volunteer at Yellowstone before moving on to college.

"I just thought I would really enjoy this. And, man, did I make the right decision," Phil said proudly.

"My dad once kicked me out of the house and dropped me off in Wisconsin Dells to find a job when I was your age," I stated, regretting where I ended up, instead of the reason for being kicked out in the first place. "Don't get me wrong, I deserved it, but this would have been the best punishment ever, if only I had known about it."

"Yeah," Phil laughed. "It is pretty awesome. They feed and house hundreds of us all in different situations. People reflecting on their own lives, or just taking a break from the hustle of the city in one of the most amazing places around. Of course, we all have to work, but it's a pretty big win/win for everyone."

I wished I knew about the programs Yellowstone offered when I was his age. I could tell Phil loved every second of it. I was glad that he had found Yellowstone, as being surrounded by such robust natural beauty would surely help him grow into a strong individual with good character.

We had a pleasant conversation with Phil, and by the end of our meal we were debating on waiting out the storm or returning to the motorcycle to ride back to camp in the rain without our helmets.

In Phil's past six months in the park, he was beginning to catch on to the weather patterns. He said that even though the sky was a mass of black clouds at the moment, they would be clearing up to a cloudless dusk in less than an hour.

Marisa and I figured we would wait out the storm, and to our surprise, forty-five minutes later the sky was the clearest it had been all day. The absence of clouds now let the stained-glass heavens show off their colorful lights as a grand finale to the day.

We said our goodbyes to Phil, walked back to the bike, and returned to our temporary home to absorb the day's bewilderment. It had been a long day filled with astonishing sights that would not be forgotten.

We crawled into our tent, inflated the air mattress until it was once again full, glanced at the next day's priorities, and drifted off to the sounds of nature, and the scuffle of people walking by our tent to use the bathroom.

Badlands National Park / South Dakota

The Black Hills / South Dakota

Devil's Tower / Wyoming

Tim at the summit of Beartooth Pass (10,947 ft.) / Montana

Yellowstone, Wyoming

Tim overlooking Yellowstone River / Wyoming

Marisa at Yellowstone / Wyoming

Bryce Canyon National Park / Utah

Arches National Park / Utah

Delicate Arch, Arches National Park / Utah

Colorado River in Moab / Utah

La Sal Mountain Loop Road / Moab, Utah

Lunar landscape of RT-12 to Escalante, Utah

Notch Mountain, Rocky Mountain National Park / Colorado

Chapter 7 - Faithful

A mysterious glow through the east side of the tent woke me up the next morning. I unzipped the flap of the tent and took a curious peek for the source.

"Hey, wake up!" I shook Marisa out of her slumber.

"What's going on, what happened?" she asked in a panic.

I threw open the tent door.

"Ta-da! Nothing but blue skies, baby!" I proclaimed with pride, not that I had anything to do with it.

The trend of waking up to an overcast sky was over. The sun was rising in all its glory from behind the hills.

A look at the day's forecast did show cloud coverage building up around noon, and there was a chance of rain throughout the afternoon (of course), but starting the day off with clear skies and some sunshine could really set the mood for the day.

I went through my routine of making coffee, because I am utterly useless until I have caffeine in my system. Marisa, on the other hand, had her tea, because she is much more civilized than I. We boiled more water so she could have her oatmeal to jump start her body to the same effect coffee alone has on me.

The day's agenda was intentionally loose. Since my last and only other visit to Yellowstone was when I was nine, I did not recall the exact locations of all the main sights we wanted to visit, but Old Faithful was a must. I also vaguely remembered Mammoth Hot Springs as being absolutely awe-inspiring.

We set off west, sun to our backs, and were at Old Faithful in no time. This famous geyser erupted every hour and a half to two hours and had been doing so long before it was discovered in 1870.

A crowd had already been waiting close to ninety minutes when we claimed a spot on the long benches that guaranteed us a front-row seat.

With growing anticipation for the spectacle that was about to take place before us, we readied every recording device we had. The phones, the GoPro knockoff, and our actual camera were all on standby.

Marisa and I both sat, ready to press record for what seemed like another half hour before the ground started gurgling. Small jets of steamy water burst into the air, signaling it was time. Then, in one giant eruption, the geyser spat boiling water a hundred feet into the sky.

I filmed for two full minutes before I realized I was staring at a screen instead of the unfiltered, real deal, directly in front of me. I promised I would devote my full attention to the Cirque du Soleil of nature from that point on.

With the geyser dying down to a sputter, we tried to beat the retreating crowd as people often do in the bottom of the ninth inning at baseball games. It seemed this was the new standard, and we would have met less traffic if we had left at the end, instead of just before. I kicked myself for being such a sheep.

Even though we had no set schedule for the day, I knew the latter part of the day all depended on how fast we got to Mammoth Springs. I was back into a take-your-time-but-hurry-up attitude.

On the way north we saw points of interest we would like to explore on the way back, and started making a mental list. That list turned out to be just about everything on the way, but we tried to stick to our guns and ride all the way up to Mammoth Springs uninterrupted.

The road was surrounded by magnificent waterfalls, grand rock formations, and steaming geyser basins. Huge flats of earth were riddled with sulfuric pools.

These temptations became just too great for any nature-loving human to simply drive by with only the possibility of seeing them later. So we rolled the dice on seeing Mammoth Springs in favor of the marvels we kept passing on the way.

There were a couple of branches off the main road that dipped into intimate, less-traveled offshoots, that reconnected back to the main road after a short distance. We pulled into one of these side roads on a whim: Firehole Lake Drive.

The narrow one-way drive was built into the side of a deep canyon. It seemed we had passed through an unknown portal, separating us from the congested traffic of the rest of the park, into a paved version of the Inca Trail.

A wide, wild river roared in and out of sight to our right. Angry white caps shot mist into the air as the water crashed against the boulders that refused to budge against the current. I couldn't hear anything over the sound of the river, but I was sure if it was muted, we would be able to hear the mating calls of howler monkeys and pumas growling in the scenery around us.

The drive followed the rapids of the river and ended at a cluster of cascading waterfalls. With no cars in sight, we parked in the middle of the road to appreciate this hidden gem.

Firehole Lake Drive was only five or six miles, but it inspired us to take any available secondary offshoots we came across. With everyone's attention on getting from one attraction to the next via the main road, this drive was evidently not traversed as often as it should have been.

Advancing north, we were again emotionally forced to pull over despite the many miles that lay ahead, due to the presence of a giant waterfall called Gibbon Falls. This gigantic drop was a hundred feet taller than the previous falls we had just seen. The water tumbled down the rocks violently, only to return to the peace and calm of the slumbering river snaking off into the grand vastness of the green valley in the distance.

An hour and a half south of Mammoth Springs, the last leg of our ride was filled with roads winding through the same inconceivable terrain we learned to expect from this national park of wonders. Once we finally reached our destination at the northwest section of the park, the pressure of the day lessened, having reached our second goal with a good portion of the day remaining.

Yellowstone is comprised of many different thermal formations. Geysers build up pressure in the bowels of the earth and release as fierce eruptions. Fumaroles, on the other hand, have ripped the earth's crust apart with super-heated steam, emitting gases like sulfur, giving the park its unique smell. There are also seeps: vents in the earth that slowly release extremely heated water with a high content of calcium. The calcium builds up layers over thousands of years, crescendoing skyward, creating grand pyramids and staircases.

Once again, the stills from my childhood memory were incomparable to what was physically in front of us. The tiered steps of Mammoth Springs crawled out of the earth covered in a tie-dye of colors from the algae and other microorganisms living in the heated solution. It looked like ten thousand candles in various colors had been placed randomly on different tiers, then lit to melt into the remarkable, waxy patterns on the surface we saw before us.

Most of the area was covered in crystallized calcium deposits, similar to the stuff that grows around the faucet in your bathroom sink if left unattended. In certain spots that lay atop active hot zones, there were multicolored rainbow glazes covering the stairwells. In only a few short centuries, these would also crystallize, blending into their surroundings.

The reason this was called "Mammoth Hot Springs" was that the main construction built by this process was enormous. The wooden boardwalks that led around and to the top of the structure was an hour's walk filled with complete admiration.

At last, we decided that we should head back south to check off some of the places on our mental list. There was a section of the park that had a high volume of basins, or rather, one colossally huge one split into five areas: Fountain Paint Pot, Lower Geyser Basin, Midway Geyser Basin, Biscuit Basin, and Black Sand Basin. We visited each and every one.

We followed boardwalks into fields of various sizes and colored acidic pools. The view from a helicopter must have looked like an oil painter's palette, with all the primary colors represented in individual pools, and the sporadic blending of hues in others. The temperature of each individual basin made the difference in what colors appeared, each proudly representing a unique family crest identifying the community of bacteria thriving in its own particular thermal ecosystem.

From one basin to another, we continued to be blown away. No two were alike; there were no feelings of already seen enough of those. Each one was its own mural in a gallery of fine art. We took a picture of nearly all of these phenomena, every photo a prime candidate for the cover of *National Geographic*. It felt like we could see directly into the soul of the earth through those portals.

The largest of the basins exhibited colors in a deformed bulls-eye pattern. Deep baby blues at the center, then bleach whites, emerald greens, rustic oranges, mustard yellows, and leathery browns spread across the glassy surface of the land.

We could have returned home to Illinois at that very moment with a full sense of accomplishment, and we were only on the fifth day of our journey.

The gathering clouds throughout the day had held in their daily dose of rain as long as they could bear. As we wandered the colorful basins, the clouds all detonated at once, unleashing yet another wave of showers.

We, of course, had our rain gear on hand. Marisa, in her continuous state of preparation, was already in her bright orange rain jumpsuit before the first drop landed. I, on the other hand, had to quickly remove my leather jacket and dig through my bag to put on my own wardrobe of woes.

I wanted to test to see if the weather was at all influenced by the number of teeth I had closed on the zipper of my rain jacket. I was sure that if I zipped my jacket all the way to the collar, the sun would come out in all its glory, but with every tooth unclasped, the moisture in the air would collect, forming darker and darker clouds. And if completely unzipped and removed, it would be guaranteed to rain.

With the sun setting behind the clouds, and the rain coming down, we rode at a moderate pace back to our campsite. It would have taken effort not to have had an amazing day, but ours was above and beyond any we could have hoped for.

Once back at our tent, we crawled inside to view some of the pictures we had taken to confirm the sights that we'd seen were real.

As Marisa and I laid on top of our air mattress, we daydreamed about future trips and where we might go. She had already traveled more of the world than I could ever hope to.

Part of this excitement sparked a conversation about future traveling, what was needed to do so, and what was impossible. Her career as a teacher with open summers was a fundamental piece of the puzzle, and the fact that we did not have children was a current convenience.

I personally had yet to feel the need or want to have a child, so this was a tricky subject with Marisa, because one day she did want to bear a child. It was a fragile subject that had been discussed before, and I was sure it would have to be talked about at length between us again.

Marisa explained that she wanted to take our children on trips similar to the ones my father took me on. To places like the one we were at now, or getting lost on purpose through the woods of Minnesota, like I did with my mother. All of those excursions rooted deep memories that built character in me and added mystery to the world.

As I told Marisa nonchalantly of the amazing trips I went on with my parents as a child, she directly correlated my stories, as well as her own adventures through life, with places we could go with our own children.

Our discussion got intense pretty quickly. Like, on a supernova level.

Marisa turned to face me, her eyes stone serious and firm. "Then just tell me once and for all, do you ever want to have children or not?"

I sighed, knowing this was not going to end well. "I don't know. I can't say I don't ever want children, who knows what the future holds. But at the moment, no." I watched her expression melt with disappointment. "What I do know is that I've always been faithful, and I love our life as it is now and don't want any drastic changes."

"Well, are you ever going to ask me to marry you?" she asked.

My heart started racing in my chest. "Will having children be a defining factor in your response?" I countered.

"I don't know," she replied, and with glassy eyes turned to gaze away from me.

It broke my heart. We were caught in the moment of a real crappy conversation, all initiated by the fantastic day we had. It did not make sense.

"We're messing everything up," I said in frustration.

And with that, we both went to bed very unhappy campers.

Chapter 8 - Engaging Scenery

The next morning's weather matched our moods. It was dark, grey, and drizzling. After our lovely chat the night before, we stubbornly kept to ourselves, barely talking to each other.

We both knew this type of conduct could not continue, but it was Marisa who made the peace offering of friendly casual conversation and sincere smiles.

"Tim, I really want today to be just as special as what we've experienced together throughout this last week. I'm having the time of my life, and I don't want it all to be tarnished by a ten-minute argument."

Her heartfelt statement cut deep through my layers of anger and hard-headedness.

I replied, "I want today to be amazing too, and I'm truly sorry for being such an ass last night."

"I'm sorry too. We can't let such hateful words and behavior take over and threaten to ruin our trip," she said, smiling back at me.

"Well, it's a brand-new day, so let's start it off on the right foot." I leaned in and kissed her, truly not wanting any hostile feelings lingering throughout the day.

After our morning routine of coffee, tea, and breakfast, we headed back out into the park with the best intentions of having another great day, and with the hopes of a slightly different ending.

The day before, we had concentrated our sightseeing to the western side of the giant figure-eight that made up the park's main roadway system. Today was our last full day, and we rode off to explore the eastern side of the park.

There was only one place I absolutely had to visit that day, one I had researched extensively prior to our trip. It was in the same neighborhood as another tightly-grouped cluster of attractions about two hours away from our campground.

As our mood began to return to that of civil people, the skies retracted their threatening and hostile fronts as well. We rode alongside Lake Yellowstone once again, triggering the same reactions as the first time we saw its beauty coming into the park.

The sun was just rising over the mountain range on the other side of the lake as we rode past. A huge mushroom-shaped cloud rose straight into the air and flattened outward against the lower levels of the atmosphere. The combination of the clouds with the sun directly behind them looked as if an atomic bomb had just been set off.

A hundred yards into the lake was a small rock protruding out of the water. The rock must have had some elements of dirt to it, because out of this modest-size rock, emerged a fairly large tree. I loved the thought that even on the smallest patch of cramped real estate, a tenacious little tree was able to poke its head into the world and look around. Nature truly had an open-door policy for life.

Marisa and I talked to each other in good spirits, pointing out what we saw around us and genuinely enjoying each other's company. It was a very peaceful forty-five-minute drive along the coast.

An hour north of the lake we began to catch glimpses of the Yellowstone River. After thousands of years, the river had cut deep into the earth in what is now known as the Grand Canyon of Yellowstone.

On our way into the park two days prior, we had pulled over onto an overlook to see this same canyon and river without knowing their names at the time. Now, armed with a map, we could identify what we had already seen and what was yet to be discovered.

We spotted two sections of the road that looked like they might be on par with Firehole Lake Drive, the intimate little road that led us to the cascading falls. The roads were on opposing sides of the Grand Canyon of Yellowstone, plainly named North Rim Drive and South Rim Drive.

Both roads gave different vantage points of the same two waterfalls of the Yellowstone River, simply named Upper and Lower Falls. It seemed there was not a whole lot of creativity involved in naming these attractions. We headed for North Rim Drive on the east side of the canyon first.

This was another one of the defining moments when I was glad I was on a motorcycle. With my head raised high in the air, without the constrictions of windows, or being wrapped in metal, I had a clear panoramic view of the astounding landscape surrounding us. As we pulled into the main loop of North Rim Drive, it was apparent that this wasn't a secluded section of the park, but one of the main attractions.

The jaw-dropping views overlooking the canyon could not be kept secret. The busy one-way road followed the very edge of the canyon. There was only a small stone barrier separating us from a drop-off to certain doom down the canyon to the river far below.

Thankfully there were pull-offs, because I didn't feel I was getting my fair share of the engaging scenery since I was piloting the bike. So, we pulled over and walked onto a platform overhanging the canyon.

As we approached the canyon's edge, we heard the faint roaring of the falls in the distance. When we peaked over the railing into the canyon, our field of vision sprung to life in full animation. Whole communities of turkey vultures, osprey, and eagles flew in long sweeping circular patterns. They built nests in every available nook and cranny in the faces and peaks of the canyon.

The canyon was a classic "Y" shape that dropped swiftly to the rapids of the river below. The walls were splashed with limestone as white as snow. The reflective rays of the sun made the stone twinkle like far away galaxies plastered onto the canyon's sides. The remaining colors of the surface were horizontal layers of red, pink, orange, and of course yellow. The canyon was literally rusting from the iron within the stone itself. It was an absolute marvel to take in.

We stood on the deck in silence looking at the river below with the waterfall in the distance, and the brilliant colors of the canyon. We were both deep inside our individual subconscious, absorbing the phenomenal panorama in our own ways.

There are moments in time that suddenly shift us for the better, moments that make us realize how small we are in the world, and how insignificant our individual lives are that span just a short amount of time. We come to be, we die, and then we are forgotten. For most, this process doesn't take more than 150 years to play out to the completely-and-utterly-forgotten stage. To squabble with loved ones and ruin mornings, days, or even weeks over skirmishes seemed so trivial in the grand scheme of things.

Obviously, I was having a very un-masculine moment, and I was trying to keep it to myself, but I privately pledged to be more patient with Marisa when she was having trouble reading my mind, or if we didn't agree on something a hundred percent, to maybe let her get her way every once in a while.

Those dainty and tender feelings were only byproducts of the raw emotions created from being truly inspired by my surroundings. I was certain they would pass naturally without the need of porn, football, or alcohol to regenerate my testosterone, but I really wanted to be sure I remembered how much I loved and cared for Marisa.

Tempted by what other sights might still be out there, we carried on down the road that followed the canyon. We spotted a sign for Inspiration Point and turned in to see if its name held true.

Once parked, we again went to the deck built out into the canyon. The views were just as grand as the last outlook, but with different highlights from the new vantage point. We noticed a trail marker pointing down a path that led to the spot declared Inspiration Point.

Marisa and I maneuvered down a sharp descent that zig-zagged back and forth across the face of the canyon. We crossed the same creek five times at different levels of the trail. The long, steep path almost reached the base of the canyon, but stopped just short of the bottom to a deck built into the cliff's side.

The spot unquestionably lived up to its name. The lookout was parallel to the height of Upper Falls that were thundering down two hundred yards from where we stood. (44.6967925,-110.4941875) I sat on a bench facing the waterfall with my eyes fixed on the theatrics taking place before me. There was a small patch of snow to the left of the falls that the sun never seemed to be able to hit. I had seen the same splotch of white on every picture of the falls as if that snow had permanent residency.

We had the deck to ourselves. It seemed that the thousands of steps down the steep, narrow ridge proved too much for the average family. It was a good way to weed out the crowds, but we would eventually have to climb back up the laborious trial.

"This is friggin' fantastic," I finally broke the silence.

"One might say *inspirational*," Marisa said.

"I'm sure they named this place as soon as they got here," I nodded my head in the direction of the trail leading back up. "Its name might have been along the lines of 'Man-I'm-not-a-physically-fit-person Point' if they waited until after the climb back up."

Like I had feared, the hike back up took more than twice as long as the descent. With Marisa being a petite little lady, each of my lengthy strides were two of hers. We climbed at a pace we both felt comfortable with, and took little breaks as needed. I would walk a fair distance ahead and stop to wait for her to appear from around the bend, which gave me additional short intermissions. I could tell Marisa was slightly suffering from the climb at such a high altitude.

Once we finally reached the top, it was nice to rest momentarily and then get back on the bike with the only physical movement required being minor flicks of the wrist and subtle dabs with both feet.

Inspiration Point was the climax and the last available pull-off on North Rim Drive. As it was a one-way road, we now had to return to the main junction and head back down to South Rim Drive. At the end of South Rim Drive was the destination that I had researched online before our trip, a place called Artist Point.

South Rim Drive didn't cling to the side of the canyon as did its northern counterpart, but was a straight shot through a wooded area. The road ended in a giant cul-de-sac parking lot, and we found a spot conveniently close to the trail.

As we walked to the primary sidewalk, I realized I had forgotten something important on my bike, so I walked back to the bike while Marisa sat down to eat a trail bar and drink some water to recover her energy. Without her noticing, I took off the passenger seat and grabbed what was needed, then returned to Marisa who was patiently waiting for me.

The footpath immediately hooked back to the canyon's edge. The path was a wide cement walkway, intended to better serve visitors and families with little kids or the elderly.

We walked to the renowned Artist Point that I had built up to be the day's crown jewel. It was absolutely picturesque; we were along one of the bends in the canyon with a straight shot directly down the center of the river leading to an unbelievable view of Lower Falls.

The platform was crowded due to its accessibility and familiarity from being on every postcard and park brochure. The mass of people behaved respectfully as everyone took turns getting what would be the same exact picture for different photo albums around the world. The overcast skies tamed some of the colors that lived within the rocks, but the overall view was well worth the hustling hoard of people. After a few pictures, and with the platform continuously filling up with new groups of tourists, we took our leave.

Ninety-nine percent of the herd of humans ventured back to the parking lot, got in their cars, and drove off satisfied with the view. I was happy that the crowd seemed to thin out along the trails and suggested that we go down one.

The main concrete walkway ended abruptly at the lookout, but small dirt paths branched from its perimeter. I knew Marisa had just climbed the entire face of the canyon only moments ago, but I was very insistent that we go down the path into the woods that followed the canyon. Marisa smiled and pressed on.

The trail wove between the trees on a relatively flat surface with smaller segments that veined out and led to the canyon's edge. These trails were not stopped short of the actual edge by a barrier of any kind, the edge of the path was the canyon itself. Loose gravel and stones slid down the lip that continued to erode, widening the canyon ever so much each day from the rain, wind, or a careless falling hiker.

Marisa hated when I walked to the very edge of things. Not only was she genuinely concerned for my safety, but she also knew I was horrible with heights. I would lock up and freeze.

Back in Illinois at a park called Starved Rock, Marisa watched me attempt to cross a shallow gorge via a fallen tree some twenty feet in the air. I figured it would make a good photo, but as I ran out to the middle of the tree, I was struck with fear. I was deadlocked, no movement allowed. My brain switched to dumb-dumb mode. Marisa had to climb up the side and rescue me like a firefighter saving a kitten. So now I am very cautious before I walk onto any peninsulas in the sky.

Even with the risk of certain death, and being frozen by paranoia, I just had to walk out on the lip for a photo opportunity in a scenery so rare. This involved me walking out to the edge and suspending the look of terror from my face long enough for Marisa to snap a picture, and then safely stepping back to the security of solid ground.

We continued down the path until we came to a clearing in the trees for an open view of the canyon. I saw a woman walking in our direction and asked if she could take a picture of us. We walked a bit farther up the trail to a spot which I deemed acceptable for what was about to happen. Marisa stood before the outstanding background, it was perfect.

"Please press the record button," I whispered to the kind lady.

"Ok. Yep. This one here, right? Got it," she said hesitatingly.

I walked next to Marisa, posing for what she thought to be a photo. As Marisa stood smiling, standing erect in her bright orange jumpsuit, I turned to her, knelt down, pulled out the ring that had been stashed beneath the passenger seat of the bike the entire trip, and kindly requested her to marry me.

"I love you very much, and I would be honored if you would be my wife," I asked politely.

"Oh nooo … Nooo! Oh my God! Nooo! No way …" She knelt down and immediately started sobbing.

"It's the smallest ring in the world and I hope it fits." I took her hand and placed the miniscule ring on her finger.

"Nooo, it will fit and I will never take it off." She slipped it on, and it fit perfectly snug. "I love it!" She leaned in and kissed me.

Marisa appeared to be in favor of what was happening, regardless of the repetitive declarations of "no." But they turned out to be "no's" of pure shock, not the refusal of the proposal.

As previously stated, Marisa is a tiny creature of the Lord. She had long ago told me her ring size: a whopping three. This was a fact that I kept in the recesses of my mind until one day needed. I had to special order this ring size because her finger was smaller than the average twelve-year old's.

Once I received the ring, which I had sent to my father's house so that no mishaps could take place delivering it to our address, I opened the small box to see a ring that in no way would fit a grown woman.

But when the ring was presented to her, it somehow magically fit, much to my disbelief. I was very relieved.

We thanked the friendly woman caught off-guard filming our little Cinderella moment.

"That was pretty cool," the woman said as she handed me back my phone. "Be sure I got it. Oh, please say I got it."

"You nailed it!" I quickly confirmed that it recorded successfully.

In utter shock, and now in a slightly better mood, we walked beside the canyon's rim as engaged lovers. (44.720397, -110.475306)

"I am so sorry about last night," Marisa said, still wiping away her tears.

"So am I. It was a stupid conversation that got way out of hand." I hugged her deeply into my chest and kissed her forehead. "It's in the past now, and we have nothing but the future to look forward to."

It was a fairly odd coincidence that we'd had that specific conversation the night before I had planned on asking her hand in marriage, but it was a test, and we had both passed.

This was another time on our journey that as soon as our outlook on life brightened, so did the sky above. The sun came out to congratulate us and to shine light onto our newly unfolding life. We walked around a bend in the canyon to a view three times as captivating as where I decided to bend a knee, with only the sunshine now raining down on the earth.

I thought, if only I had walked a hundred more yards and waited ten more minutes, it would have been perfect. But it had been perfect, no matter the amount of light or what the location.

As we stood there absorbing the new view with a completely different outlook on life, two French gentlemen walked by. I requested a picture, and Marisa stumbled in French, stating we'd just gotten engaged. I could not understand anything but fiancé, but I saw their eyes light up once Marisa's broken French registered.

They told us they wanted to celebrate the occasion with us. One of the men fumbled through a tiny backpack to produce a bag of peanuts and smiled at us. I was very confused by this French celebratory tradition, but a moment later he presented a bottle of liquor along with two small shot glasses. I could only assume this is what any good world-traveling French hiker had stashed somewhere at hand.

The four of us had two shots each and we spoke to each other as well as we could in the mangled tongue of both languages, enjoying the moment and the view. It was a very good first encounter as an engaged couple, and I am glad we came across the two Frenchmen whose names I have forgotten, but whose kindred spirits will long be remembered.

With a little kick in our steps from the shots and the excitement behind it all, we continued down the path high on life and liquor. We sat at another ridge overhanging the canyon, Marisa taking a hundred photos of her new ring with the background matching the engravings on the ring.

Long ago at my father's house, Marisa and I were browsing through a backpacker's magazine and discussing the what-ifs of life when we randomly stumbled across an ad for rings. It turned out she was not a diamond person, thank God. The ad was by a gentleman named David Virtue who used recycled gold to create rings with beautiful landscapes. Marisa said she loved the rings and shot me a look that clearly stated, "If you ever want to buy me a ring ..."

Some designs were soft dunes, others ocean waves, and the one I picked out had mountain ranges. Each ring was handcrafted, and I was able to talk directly to Mr. Virtue himself regarding the tight timeframe, due to my indecisiveness in committing to the purchase of the ring in the months leading to our trip.

Marisa's fingers are tiny and due to the small circumference of the ring, any personalized engraving on the inside of the ring could not be many characters long. David confirmed that he, with effort, would be able to inscribe: To the Love of my Life. David met, and exceeded, my expectations. I could not have been happier with the white gold mountainous landscape on the yellow gold ring.

I was supposed to have read a little poem that I wrote for Marisa while I was on one knee, but my head went blank while I was in the moment. It was like skydiving. I knew I was doing it. It was awesome, but I was incapable of logical thought in the middle of it all. I was just going with it, and we could discuss further details after it was over.

So after a short hike further along the canyon, we sat down and I read her my poem:

From this moment on,
To the day we have grey hair and wear dentures,
I offer you this proposal. If you accept,
It will be the first of many great adventures.
They say opposites attract.
This point could not be proven finer,
Than the joining of the stars above,
Ursa Major and Ursa Minor.

We are big fans of the stars, let it be staring at them under wide-open clear skies, or watching programs on the frontiers of space on TV documentaries.

Not so long ago, it was a reoccurring joke that one day I would get a Big Dipper tattoo while Marisa got the Little Dipper. I am not sure if Marisa's mother is aware, but years ago we did in fact get these sentimental declarations permanently etched onto our skin.

My little poem, even with the timing slightly off, made Marisa very happy. We sat there and watched the video on my phone, and I discovered that after the many repetitive "no's," she had never actually said yes.

After Marisa had her fun stating the ring was a gift and it was hers regardless, she confirmed that she would indeed marry me. It was turning out to be a good day.

We took a couple of more photos deeper into the trail system, and I suggested that we head back to the general store outside of our campground to buy some spirits. I wanted to stay up as long as we could by the fire, telling stories, and staring at the thousands of white pinholes against the black canvas that made up the night sky. Marisa thought that would be a very fitting evening to wrap up the day's events.

We rode back to Grant Village's general store and purchased some of the locally brewed beers, filling both panniers with alcoholic refreshments that we would in no way be able to drink in one sitting.

When we returned to the campground, a curious neighbor walked over for small talk. I was always in the mood for friendly conversations and stories from other paths in life. So, with open beers and an open invitation, we walked across the road to meet his wife.

This was a very odd, but wonderful couple. The man was blunt and honest, short-spoken, and well into his fifties. She was a lovely Lithuanian lady around the same age. They had been married for some years now, but she spoke English as an obvious second, if not third, language with a lot of "How do you say ..." and "Forgive me for my poor English." This gentleman had not even accidentally learned any of her native tongue, but they had somehow found each other and fallen in love. It was very strange, but very cute.

Marisa, who is well versed and cultured, had a blast speaking with the woman. They shared stories of their travels that neither I, nor my newfound friend, could comment on. Neither of us had any idea of the nearest country that the story might be taking place in.

Marisa always brings an element of culture that I couldn't even begin to fake. It was nice to see her interacting with another worldly person, and I was jealous I could not bring anything to the table of intellect. I could only hope that someday I might have the smallest touch of her experiences in the world and be able to relate and connect with people in the same manner that comes so easily and charmingly to her.

We talked well into the night, telling stories of the hundreds of places we had collectively encountered, and how each fork in the road had led us to that precise moment in time.

It was wonderful hearing about the different walks of life we each chose to take. Some of which were less extensive than others, but each individual approach, course of action, and stroll through life's alleyways had brought two couples together on the smallest of all chances.

Marisa and I bid our hosts goodnight as we left to go to sleep with the world's wonders dancing in our heads, thankful for the day and all it had provided us.

Chapter 9 - Grand Tetons and Open Holes

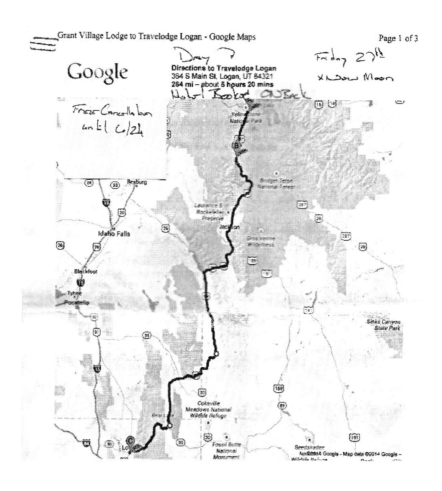

The clouds in the sky hovered like vultures preying on a half-starved man in the desert, waiting patiently for the best time to swoop down and claim its victims. Thankfully, they held off until we had packed all of our belongings into their respective containers and rolled up the tent, ready for the day's departure.

As we prepared to set off and leave Yellowstone, Marisa wrote the condensed version of the directions on her hand, beginning with a stop at the Grand Tetons Lodge to eat breakfast.

The scenery, no matter how gray, was still impressive. The sky dulled, but did not completely diminish the ride to the Tetons via US-89 S.

The initial road south was a winding path that cut through the hills and valleys with wide openings to flat plains. It did not take long for our surroundings to turn from hills into cliffs, and then evolve gradually into mountains in the near distance. The overcast sky acted as a bra on top of the Grand Tetons, the mountain range shied away from exposing its full-frontal nudity.

We stopped by the Grand Teton Lodge to sit down and have a real breakfast. As we walked up the main stairway ascending to the second floor of the lodge, we were supposed to be grandly presented with a view of the marvels of nature through the huge picture windows. Unfortunately, the haze of the world outside did not allow us the sight that John D. Rockefeller, Jr. had envisioned for us.

There were two restaurants within the lodge, and we chose to experience the less classy of the two dining options. At the countertop diner, we ate a decent-sized breakfast, and were thankful for it since we knew we had a long day of riding ahead of us.

Once fully charged, we began our trek south along US-89. The morning's ride skimmed Idaho's border, and by mid-afternoon we arrived in the fourth state we had traveled to on the KTM.

I had absolutely no expectations for Idaho. I figured we would try to ride through it quickly with the state not offering a lot to be seen along the way.

However, the southeastern portion of Idaho deeply impressed me; it was freckled with some of the same marvelous views of bluffs and cliffs we had pictured when thinking of its neighboring states. Who would have thought Idaho would be so inspiring? I felt guilty for presuming that the state's only use was producing potatoes.

We pulled over for gas in a small town that had a historic one-room schoolhouse right on the roadway. There were also exhibits and historical sites for the Oregon Trail, as well as other small wonders to be seen that brought us well into the nation's past. It was a perfect place to take a break, take a look around, stretch, and have some good-old standing up time.

One of the locals came out to greet us, offering some valuable insight as to the best route to take on our way into Logan, Utah. When I showed him our map, he confirmed that I had unintentionally chosen the best way.

We would continue on US-89, hugging the western side of Bear Lake into Logan Canyon until it spat us back out into Logan, Utah. Now confident that our course was the best way to proceed, we continued our day's ride.

We reached Bear Lake, nicknamed The Caribbean of the Rockies for its unnatural turquoise hue caused by limestone deposits suspended in the lake. It was very much like the baby blues seen at Yellowstone, but on a gigantic scale. I couldn't stop myself from continually staring at the oddity of the lake.

"Eyes on the road, love," Marisa had to keep telling me over the microphone.

Half of Bear Lake was in Idaho, the other half resided in Utah. We continued to ride south down the western side of the lake until US-89 broke off from the waterfront and headed directly into Utah.

It seemed as soon as we had entered Idaho, we'd left it only moments later. I was glad that we had cut the corner of the state and now gained newfound respect for it.

By entering Utah, we had arrived in the fifth state via the motorcycle. It was a good feeling piling up the list of states we rode through on the KTM.

With the lake now in our side mirrors, we were faced head-on with the Uinta-Wasatch-Cache National Forest. This began yet another road that would last the test of time in my memories.

Deeply cut, almost vertical limestone walls greeted us as we entered the canyon. The scenic byway ran parallel to a winding river which crawled through the gorge. The overcast sky robbed us of many of the environment's astonishments, but there were momentary glimpses through clear patches of sky to distant mountain peaks tipped with brilliant gold and red crowns. I was sure we would return to experience the same ride on a clear and sunny day at another point in my traveling career.

Marisa thought the foggy mist added a certain tranquility to the scenery and would not have changed it given the choice. I was glad she was there snapping pictures and enjoying the ride for all its worth, regardless of the weather. She was a hard one to disappoint and always had a positive outlook on life in any circumstance.

While we continued down the road, Marisa and I started to play a game of riddles we made up. Every answer was based on puns ending with the word "tea." We're a weird couple, but it passed the time.

"What type of tea did Jesus drink?" I questioned.

"Spirituali-tea!" Marisa proclaimed, sure that she nailed it.

"I will accept that, but I would have also accepted Christiani-tea." I gave her half a point.

"Alright, what type of tea drives you crazy?"

I thought about it for a moment. "Insani-tea!"

"You got it." A full point was awarded to me.

"What type of tea killed the cat?" I said sadly, immediately thinking of our two cats we left at home.

"Curiosi-tea!" she laughed as she answered.

We continued to play until we both ran out of spontaneous tea puns. There are plen-tea of them out there, but we saved some for our next battle of the minds.

We reached the top of a hill and saw the town of Logan far off in the distance, only to disappear again once the road descended back into the canyon.

A short distance later we entered a valley completely commercialized into the bustling urban community of Logan. The town was surrounded by outstanding views in every direction. I was very jealous of the community and their opportunity to explore the nature immediately around them at any given moment.

We cruised up and down the main road and finally found our motel. Unfortunately, the hotel had conveniently changed ownership since I booked it online, and therefore the original name had been covered with a giant temporary banner displaying the new name. There was no email sent to let me know, it was just a case of figure it out for yourself.

Regardless of the confusion, it had been four nights since our last hotel room, and we took advantage of the room's heater and shower to its maximum potential.

After utilizing the technologies of a modern facility, we set off to explore the town and get something to eat. Being completely unfamiliar to our surroundings, we figured we would walk around to see what we could stumble across on foot.

We walked down a side street that branched off the main strip and decided to see how Utah pizza stood against our beloved Chicago style we were so proud of (not really).

We found a diner called The Factory Pizzeria. Its main entrance was a stairwell squeezed between what looked to be the same Italian restaurant wrapped around both sides. The Pizzeria was a basement establishment directly underneath the Italian restaurant.

Our eyes had to adjust to the low lighting, and once they did, we realized most would have considered it to be a dive. Peanut shells and popcorn littered the floor and our shoes slightly stuck to the ground from spilt pop. In other words, my kind of pizza joint.

They had anything and everything I could ever want to eat, but we decided on pizza for simplicity. After we ordered, we sat down to wait and watched some of the World Cup out of the corner of our eyes. We summarized the trip so far and went over our personal highlights.

The pizza was served in a relatively short time and the first bite convinced me that I would now have to throw away any Chicago pizza I ordered from then on. I had no idea what they put in the crust, but it was light and airy, while at the same time chewy and thick. It was insane. I was usually not judgmental when it came to food, but that pizza was crafted by saints in the image of their creator, flawless and perfect with every mouthful.

As if he had read my mind, the owner walked over and asked us how everything was.

"This is friggin' amazing! How the hell did you create the consistency of every state of matter all wrapped up into the same edible element?" I spat out my words while still chewing.

"My dad was an alchemist," he said with a wink.

"I worked at a family-run Italian joint in Chicago for five years," I said. "The pizza there was the best I ever had, up until about ten minutes ago." I kept throwing compliments at him to verify how impressed I was.

The owner thanked us for our kind words, and after we finished our meal, we headed back to our motel with full bellies and the need for a good night's rest.

The last few nights of camping we noticed that our air mattress would deflate throughout the night, and by the morning we would be in a bed taco. The middle of the mattress would end up touching the ground, instead of the buoyant six inches it should have elevated us. Clearly there was a hole somewhere that needed to be patched.

The good thing was I had thought of the possibility of this happening beforehand and had brought the patch kit that came with the mattress. I wanted to fix the problem before our next round of camping while in an environment with room to spare. But finding the hole was a much more difficult task than I had anticipated.

I inflated the mattress to capacity and crawled around on top with my ear to the surface, hoping to hear a small whistle, or feel the air slightly rushing out. I figured the hole would have originated on the bottom because that had a better chance of being punctured by sticks, rocks, or other miscellaneous objects that can wedge themselves between the ground and the bottom of the mattress.

I spent an hour flipping the mattress from its front to its back, then right-side up again. I tried folding it in half and lying on it to increase the pressure of the air escaping through the mystery hole.

"Keep digging, Watson," Marisa smirked, obviously enjoying my struggle.

"Alrighty then, Sherlock. Be my guest and break the case of the 'Muddled Mattress and the Hidden Hole.'" I was happy to pass the task onto Marisa since I was having no success and was bored with the game.

I got a kick out of watching her ever so slightly move around the mattress on all fours with her ear to the surface. It looked like she was attempting to check the heartbeat of a small beached whale.

After her patience ran out, I mounted the beast again, performing the same methodical evaluation as Marisa had. I played around with it for another half-hour, when I finally found the escape hatch that was causing us so much trouble.

It was on the top of the air mattress, not on the bottom as I'd assumed. The hole was confirmed with a wet finger placed over the suspect area. I felt the tiniest hint of cold pressure hit the moisture on my index finger. I smiled at the small personal victory.

With my weaponry of crazy glue and patches of a synthetic plastic material, I thoroughly sealed the leak. I then glued a larger square patch completely covering the new patch as well as several inches around it. I had super-glued three of my fingers together in the process, but it was a proud achievement that would ease our minds the next time we slept on the mattress.

We were both satisfied with the operation I performed on the bed, and our bellies were full of some of the best stuff on earth. We updated our Facebook pages and emailed our families. There were a lot of, "Congratulations!" floating around from my proposal.

With another successful day in the books, we slowly fell asleep to the local news.

Logan proved to be a diamond in the rough. It had originally just been a town that happened to be located at our limit of a full day's ride, but it turned out to be incredible.

Chapter 10 - Diamonds to Ruby's

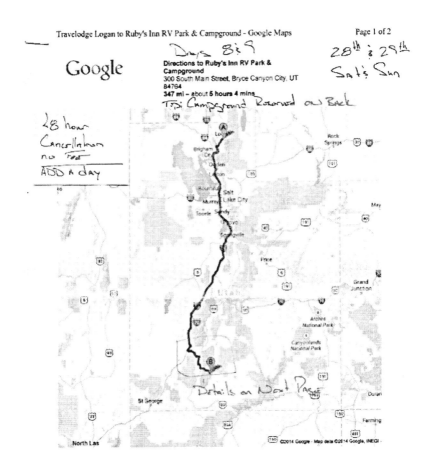

Google

Directions to Ruby's Inn RV Park & Campground
300 South Main Street, Bryce Canyon City, UT 84764
347 mi – about 5 hours 4 mins

Days 8 & 9

28th & 29th

Sat's Sun

Tipi Campground Reserved on Back

48 hour Cancellation no Fee

ADD a day

Details on Next Page

The next day's ride was a straight shot south on US-15 through Salt Lake City all the way to Bryce Canyon via UT-20 E and US-89 S.

I had originally decided we would not go any farther south than US-70 because attractions kept popping up that we would want to see, and we needed to set a limit for ourselves. If we rode to Bryce Canyon we would not be far from Zion National Park. If we rode to Zion, then we would be only a hop, skip, and a jump from the Grand Canyon.

And once we were that far south it would be a shame not to see Mesa Verde.

As the list of places we would have loved to see grew, our available time to soak them up reduced. But we did make an exception for Bryce Canyon National Park and Arches National Park. These two locations seemed to fit in just fine with our oval loop around the Rockies, and we were able to dedicate two days to each location.

After a good night's rest, we woke up to pleasant skies and packed all of our belongings back onto the bike. Today was a highway day; there were no really good ways of getting to Bryce from Logan that would have been both scenic and fast.

We knew that this was bound to happen a couple of times during the trip, but we did not look forward to highway days. Just sitting on the bike commuting took away some of the adventure spirit. But sometimes land just had to be traversed to get to the next destination.

A saving grace on days like those, and every other day we rode extensive hours on the bike, were our Airhawk seat cushions. The stock seat on the KTM was not very plush and seemed to get quite hard after only a few short hours of riding.

I had ordered an Airhawk from an online distribution center and was very pleased with the product. I could adjust the air so that my butt hovered just slightly above the seat, spreading the point of contact evenly across my derrière. Even if I added a little more air than needed, after hours of riding I could adjust it on the fly by releasing a small amount of air, giving me the feeling of a brand-new seating position.

It was very impressive and well worth the small amount of money compared to buying a custom seat. I was so happy with it, I bought one for Marisa. The cushions extended our distance traveled in comfort three-fold.

When we had been traveling around on my Yamaha Raider, Marisa had once resorted to making a handcrafted foam pad for her pillion seat. The pad was made of the type of memory foam used for pillows, and then a layer of more airy foam that would collapse under pressure. This made a stable formed seat under Marisa's weight. All of the foam was then wrapped as tightly and shapely as possible with black pleather. It technically worked, and if Marisa was happy, I, in return, was happy.

The rating for comfort was a high eight for Marisa, but the style points were closer to a two. The thing was huge. My Raider looked like a giant wasp had stung it in the rear pillion, swelling the seat to five times its normal size. It must have been a very strange sight to anyone walking by. The Airhawks were much better looking, and even more comfortable.

Marisa and I rode south on I-15 hanging out in the left lane, eating up as many miles as we could in the shortest amount of time. We were going too fast for the intercom system to work well, and the view was mostly that of the car in front of us.

And then, Salt Lake City rose from the horizon. On and off ramps slowed down traffic due to the local business congestion of the city. To our left was another giant backdrop of a beautiful mountainous landscape, the foreground a modern city. I had never paid attention to the finer details of the pictures I had previously seen of Salt Lake City and was now blown away by its majestic location and surroundings.

We needed gas and a break from the highway, so we pulled off at an exit halfway through the city. By chance we saw a Ducati and Triumph dealer, so we pulled in to see if they could fix my broken horn.

"It will be a couple hours," said one of the mechanics. "There's a KTM dealer a couple exits down the highway. You may have better luck there."

I did not want to wait hours and delay the day for a simple fix, so we headed to the KTM dealership to see if they could squeeze in a warranty repair for a pair of travelers far from their local dealership.

I had noticed that one of the two wires running into the horn had broken free. It was too tight for me to bandage myself, so I was hoping that with a pair of wire snippers and a crimper they could repair the wires and send us back out on our way in a short amount of time.

And it was just that. After a small explanation, a young man rolled our fully loaded bike into the shop, and ten minutes later brought it back out.

"You're good to go, brother," he said with a smile. "Good as new!"

Not a penny spent. With a couple of reassuring honks of the horn, we took back off onto I-15 South with a fully functional machine, genuinely pleased with KTM.

Ever since we left Logan, we had been traveling just west of the Uinta-Wasatch-Cache National Forest and its inspiring views. Even though the day was 80 percent on US-15, there was still plenty to look at in the distance: snow-capped mountains and clumps of forests staggered just beyond the road's edges.

Once we got farther south, the landscape began to change dramatically. The mountains receded and gave way to dry, rocky hills full of browns, pinks, and sand-colored stone. When we split off US-89 South onto UT-12, the ride started to get real interesting.

We twisted through roads that had giant red rock sculptures staggering from one side of us to the other. The road hugged the side of a giant wall that emerged out of the ground displaying its technicolor dreamcoat of reds, browns, and oranges. The thick rock proved it had stood the test of time over tens of thousands of years, and would be around for at least as long as it already had in that same solid formation.

Then, out of nowhere we rode directly under a stone arch spanning the width of the two-lane road. It reminded me of the old photos of cars driving through a hole burrowed through a great sequoia tree. And just around the corner we road through another arch formation that crossed high above our heads.

"This is insane," I whispered to myself, but Marisa caught it on the mic.

"It's incredible," Marisa whispered back.

Mile after mile we continued down the road paved through the heart of the most bizarre landscape. It was too much; it was everything I could have wanted, and it rekindled every emotion of adventure and excitement I had felt long before setting off on this trip, or while jealously reading other people's travelogues of the world.

Marisa and I might not have been in some remote location in Africa, but we were far from home and wouldn't have traded places with anyone else in the world. (37.741148, -112.299752)

We continued through the gardens of rock for another three miles, and the red cliffs seemed to melt away back into the earth. We were only five or so miles from our campground at Ruby's Inn just outside of Bryce Canyon, and it was becoming sweltering hot.

I felt very comfortable for the first time in days that the likelihood of rain was near zero percent. With the rain suit long ago taken off, I was finally able to ride in just my leather jacket, and that was uncomfortably hot on its own, even with all of the vents and front zipper open. I could not wait to unpack the bike and be rid of the more cumbersome articles of clothing I had layered on.

Marisa and I pulled in to Ruby's Inn to find it was more of a commercialized town than just a hotel and campground. We rode down the main street that included gas stations, a car wash, general stores, souvenir shops, a laundromat, ATV rentals, and its own post office. It was kind of tacky, but not unreasonably so. It had been built with an old western feel to it without going overboard.

As we pulled over to check in, I had a little surprise for Marisa. We were going to stay in a tipi for the next two nights, and I knew she would love it.

We registered and rode to our tipi. It had a giant brown turkey painted on its side. Marisa's eyes lit up as she ran inside.

"Oh my God, oh my God, oh my God," she kept repeating excitedly, as she ran around the interior of the tipi like the turkey stamped on the canvas outside.

"Thought you might like it," I stated, clearly underestimating her reaction.

"Like it? I love it! This is going to be so awesome!" she said, still exploring the tipi as if it had four rooms and an upstairs bathroom.

"I'm just glad we don't have to mess around with the tent for a couple of days," I joked.

Marisa was a tipi connoisseur. She actually built a tipi in Colorado and lived in it for a couple of months. Trust me when I say this girl has done everything.

Once thoroughly inspected, she gave it her final approval and kissed me on the cheek.

The tipi was definitely not a cheaply thrown-together replica of what one would assume a tipi might be in a tourist town. The construction was authentic in every way Marisa pointed out, from two staggered layers of canvas for the circulation of air, to the round door that had to be rolled up with sticks and leather strings to remain open.

Marisa was very pleased, and her excitement fueled my enthusiasm.

Once we unloaded all of our goods, inflated the patched-up mattress, and made the bed, I went off to fetch two bottles of water from the general store.

There was a young woman in front of me checking in as I waited patiently, looking at the gizmos and gadgets they sold. Once her business was conducted, she walked out of the store.

Then the lady behind the counter looked me dead in the eyes and asked me very politely, "Was that woman wearing any pants or underwear?"

"Ummmm ..." I had to think back for a mental image of the woman who was just in front of me. "I'm usually pretty good at spotting public nudity, but I honestly can't confirm or deny," I told the woman behind the counter. I was upset my attention had been diverted from the suspect below-the-waist streaker.

"I don't think she had any pants on. I can't wrap my mind around it," the cashier said confused.

I paid for my bottles of water and returned to our tipi, disappointed that I had missed out on witnessing something potentially fantastic.

Our tipi was the second in a row of three and I saw that the first tipi was now occupied. Our new neighbors were a group of promiscuously dressed girls in their twenties or early thirties at best. I spotted the nudist in question and laughed to myself as I noticed she was wearing skin-colored nylon shorts, tight-as-could-be with fake tattoos printed on them. She indeed looked to be walking around flaunting her lady parts.

She was one of four girls unpacking their luggage from a rental car. I tried not to stare at the group of what my mind only presumed to be a flock of traveling lesbian strippers. I was only on the second day of being engaged, but my mind immediately raced to the plot of any poorly scripted porno. I wiped my mind clean and ran back into our tipi.

"We have neighbors." I tried to hide the excitement in my voice. "We should really make an attempt to hang out with them."

"Awesome! Sounds fun," Marisa replied.

"It does sound fun," I whispered.

Unfortunately, the neighboring girls were busy unpacking, and we only had a few hours of daylight left to see any of the sights of Bryce Canyon before the sun set.

So with our luggage unpacked and now wearing only a T-shirt, my leather jacket, and a loose pair of jeans, we planned to enter Bryce Canyon on the bike and ride the full length of the eighteen-mile road until it dead-ended at Rainbow Point. We'd get to snap some pictures and then have enough daylight to make it back to the tipi.

We mounted the KTM and headed off into the unknown. We were riding down the road in the middle of a giant plateau that stretched out in both directions as far as the eye could see. The gentle hills in every direction spread across the land like waves on a calm lake, and the slanted sunlight pierced through gaps in the evergreens that surround the road.

But then the casual road that climbed gradually through the forest abruptly changed. As we rode along, we noticed the forest to our left dissipate, and then, all at once the edge of the canyon emerged in all its glory.

We immediately pulled over to soak in the view.

The green hills behind us covered in pine trees marched all the way up to the very edge of the plateau. Some of the trees overflowed onto the side of the canyon like water that burst through a dam. The colors changed from the greens of the trees blanketing the earth behind us, only to be overthrown by the now predominant reds and oranges of the barren rock in front of us.

Not only did the colors change, but the hills that once looked to be gentle waves flowing across the landscape, now looked as if Zeus had thrown a boulder into a lake, shattering its peaceful stillness. Shafts of red earth shot into the sky from within the deformed landscape.

I could only assume that this new terrain had been created by a process of immense violence and shaking of the earth, when in reality, it turned out to be the peaceful process of erosion that had slowly created the spectacular views before us.

The sun was out, the weather was perfect, and I was continuously being battered with the most amazing sight I had ever seen from one pull-off to the next.

God, was it amazing. My oldest brother told me he had spent a couple of weeks at Bryce in his twenties, just walking around digesting all of its wonders. Indeed, there is no place on earth that I have experienced quite like Bryce Canyon.

The road climbed higher and higher along the cliff's edge as the plateau rose in altitude, and every pull-off was its own world wonder. It was eighteen miles of complete bliss.

We made it all the way to the end of the road to Rainbow Point, where there was a grand view looking out over the panoramic landscape. (37.475359, -112.240512) It was a vista of everything we had seen all at once, filled with all the components of the individual pull-offs that we observed while riding up, now combined into one masterpiece.

A little plaque stated that on the clearest of days, you could see all the way to the North Rim of the Grand Canyon. With squinty eyes and the fullest concentration, I couldn't be sure if any of the dips and drops in the distance were in fact the Grand Canyon or not. "I don't know what the hell we are looking at, but this is crazy," I said awestruck.

"It's beautiful," Marisa said just as amazed as I was.

It was incredible how the earth seemed to shoot up out of nowhere into the sky in sudden and massive surges. I loved having no idea how Bryce Canyon, Devil's Tower, or any of the madness that made up Yellowstone could have ever come to be.

I liked to believe, briefly, that it was some magical force, and to let my mind wonder, never being able to come up with any logical explanations. Then, only after my mind had had its fun with nature's Rubik's Cube, I read the little plaques that conveyed the most elite scientist's explanation. And sometimes even those experts stated that their conclusion was still only a best guess at what lay before them.

Bryce Canyon was not a typical canyon made by the erosion of a river cutting through it. Rather, the canyon had been made over millions of years by frost wedging, along with wind and water erosion.

The temperature there waxes and wanes around the point of freezing over 200 times a year. So any moisture in the stone acts like tiny crowbars prying open and breaking off rocks from the main plateau. The winter invites melting snow into the openings, and like the potholes in the road around any major city, they begin to widen with the force of nature.

This process turned the plateau into narrow rows of earth called fins, which eroded from within, developing windows. The windows then fully eroded, leaving tall standing columns of stone called hoodoos. The whole creation procedure from arches and windows to hoodoos could be seen step by step within the same field of view.

Satisfied with the day, we headed back down the eighteen-mile stretch to our tipi. Our plan was to explore the many different intersecting trails of Bryce Canyon the following morning after a good night's rest. We wanted to get up as early as possible before the heat's reign could terrorize us under the midday sun.

Once we exited the park, I noticed ATV trails branching off the main road, and I wanted to test my bike's capabilities as well as my own off-roading skills once again. So we turned onto one of the entrances that funneled through the forest on a gravel road.

There were no ATV trails in the National Park itself, to avoid excessive erosion from human traffic, but these trails lay just on the outskirts in the forested plateau and went through some interesting terrain.

I was still new to the whole off-road riding experience and had a lovely passenger sitting directly behind me, so I did not push my skills to any limit. But I rode around standing up and going over the semi-loose gravel with no problems at all.

We came to our first rookie obstacle: an incline in the gravel road much steeper than anything I had ever ridden on. I managed to carefully ride up the incline through the loose gravel with the front tire bouncing around only slightly, but it was enough to grow my fears of dropping my bike with its precious cargo: Marisa.

"So, this is fun and all, but can we please go back to the tipi?" Marisa said, challenging my skill level.

"Yes," I replied in defeat, but was glad to quit while I was ahead.

She dismounted the bike, not wanting anything to do with the ride back down the hill I had so triumphantly conquered, and headed down by foot to meet me at the bottom.

I readied the action camera to its mount on the handlebars so people could witness my achievement at a later time. I just knew this was going to be epic.

I rode the brakes the whole way down, not really having any control in the path I took, but I reached the bottom and turned my head, grinning at Marisa who continued walking down the slope to meet me.

"I did it!" I told her with pride.

"You did awesome," she said, keeping my confidence high. She got back on the bike, and we rode back to the intersection with the paved road leading to our tipi.

We later watched the video of me and my daring ride down the hill of hell, only to see that what looked to be a monstrosity in the moment, was instead a child's bunny hill. The excitement behind ever showing anyone the large task I overcame faded as I watched myself ever-so-unsteadily descending a small gravel bump in the landscape.

It was no hill of epic proportion. Any twelve-year-old on a motocross bike would have shimmied up or down it going forty miles an hour comfortably. I figured the telling of the story verbally would be grander in effect than the video could ever reflect.

The two of us sat on the picnic table discussing the day and the plan for tomorrow as our neighbors walked around their tipi in their half-naked state of existence. Marisa said I should invite them over, but I was too nervous, like a nerd talking to cheerleaders in junior high.

"Don't be a dork, just invite them over," Marisa prompted.

"You do it," I begged.

"Stop acting like an idiot and invite them over," she said, seeing I was uncomfortable for no apparent reason.

I only imagined that these women had a very different lifestyle than ourselves, but even so, I was sure we could find enough commonalities to have an entertaining night with some beers.

I finally gathered enough courage to say with a wave, "Hey, neighbors," without my voice cracking. And two of them even walked over to our campsite.

They were very exotic-looking creatures, and we settled into the small talk that occurs when first meeting people. Despite their looks, these two ladies were much more down to earth than I had assumed, and we made a date for a night full of drinking and conversation.

Our new friends had been traveling with a full bar stocked between three coolers during their trip, but Marisa and I had to run to the general store to participate in this mass consumption of alcohol. We stocked up on some fancy beers, went back to our tipi, and took a short nap in preparation for our night's activities.

We woke up well relaxed and with the strength needed to drink and be sociable neighbors. The girls all came over as I was starting a fire. They were well-equipped with bottles of vodka, Bloody Mary mixes, and a cooler filled with a variety of beers. We got right down to business and found ourselves all enjoying each other's company in moments.

I told Heather, the woman who was dressed in the flesh colored skin-tight nylons, about the lady behind the counter trying to verify ever so politely if she had been wearing any pants.

We all laughed hysterically as the girls confirmed they were indeed getting some strange looks from people walking and driving by. I held in my mental comments that I assumed they were all strippers and I was one of the people looking at them with confusion.

It turned out that they were not in fact a traveling horde of lesbian strippers from Vegas, but just a group of girls from Portland, Oregon, on a cross-country vacation. One last trip before they all found themselves scattered across the country with time-consuming jobs or children in their adult lives.

It was awesome that these four young women all squeezed into a rental car to explore the openness of the west before life got too busy for such journeys. They told us about where they had been and where they planned to go before they had to retreat back to their normal lives.

We, in turn, told them the up-to-date story of our travels. Marisa flaunted her ring, and all of the girls got emotional. I was surrounded

by estrogen, but the story made me look like a good guy, so I let them all 'ooh' and 'aah' me for proposing.

The night carried on, and the drinks went down easily as we all shared good chuckles over our individual explorations. Late into the night the ladies bid us goodnight and disappeared back into their campsite. It did not take long for Marisa and me to settle onto our air mattress and pass out completely exhausted and satisfied from the day's activities.

Chapter 11 - Constellation Prize

Waking up the following day took a little more effort than the average morning. I had to drink some extra cups of coffee to reboot my body into adventure mode. A nice warm shower also helped revitalize my spirits. The plan was to get lost within the hoodoos and hoo-don'ts on a three-and-a-half-mile hike in the heart of Bryce Canyon.

We filled up our water bottles and stripped down to shorts and T-shirts in preparation for the midday heat that would inevitably come. We packed a lunch of junk food and sandwiches purchased from the general store for an afternoon break somewhere along the trail.

Fully packed, and only moderately hung over, we rode into the canyon towards Sunrise Point to then hike the Queen's Garden Trail.

I knew that without doing any research beforehand, the park's seemingly unlimited amount of trail systems could have been overwhelming. I doubted that any choice would have led to disappointment, but I wanted a refined list that highlighted the key areas we should see with only a day in the park to explore.

My research showed that Queen's Garden Trail was at the top of the list. It merged and bled into other trails that, depending on one's stamina, made it possible to choose one's own adventure from multiple options, including pressing forward or retreating back up the three-hundred-and-twenty-foot canyon wall.

Bryce Canyon was truly a garden of the gods. The trail began by treating us to views overlooking the canyon's length. We found ourselves stopping to take in the view of every unique red structure that stretched into the sky, each one having its own fingerprint that differed slightly from the rest of the formations.

We looked at the pillars on a personal, individual basis, with the background filled in with thousands more of the beautiful columns. We were in no hurry and had the entire day to roam around at our own pace, so we took every opportunity to just stare out for five minutes every fifty feet or so at each new slide of scenery.

While Marisa and I hiked through the narrow, rocky trails on the side of a deep slope of loose gravel, we came upon two Evel Knievel inspired kids in their teens. The two juveniles were trying to make

their presence known to everyone around them by loudly discussing the best way to descend directly down the side of the giant slope.

"Hey, Bradley, check it out. Wouldn't it be totally badass if we got down to that landing?"

"Nah, broseph, we should head over to that ledge. It looks extreme, but we got this!"

I half expected them to blurt out, "Party on, Wayne. Party on, Garth," and high five.

None of the other hikers were impressed by their shenanigans either, but were instead annoyed by the boys' blunt disrespect for the park and the signs clearly stating to stay on the paths to reduce the erosion process, as well as to ensure the extended lifespan for any mindless hiker.

But of course, Tweedle Dum and Tweedle Dumber proceeded to get down on all fours in a reverse crab position. They scooted down on their rear ends, which did not look as extreme as they had probably been hoping, as rocks tumbled down in front of them in their quest for glory.

We did not give them the attention they were so desperately seeking and hoped that we would not hear in the hours to come about some tragic event circulating through the park due to these boys' careless actions.

Our descent was far less challenging than theirs, but still took effort and concentration while navigating through the loose gravel on the steep hills. Once we reached the bottom by following the switchbacks that swooped down the side of the canyon wall, we got a whole new perspective of the monuments surrounding us.

Instead of looking down into the landscape, we were now looking up and outward, humbled by the enormity and oddity of the environment. It was absolutely out of this world. Marisa had been to some pretty exotic places on this planet, but for me, the thousands of tall red monoliths were too strange for reality.

I firmly believed that if someone plucked up a sleeping subject from any other place in the world, and then somehow transported them to the exact location where we stood, then woke them up and scurried off, they would no doubt think they had been abducted by aliens and were now on a foreign planet. I almost felt that way, and I had ridden there from my house.

The contrast in colors surrounding us was brilliant. The sky was deep blue with perfect puffs of white clouds. There were bright greens in the trees and bushes that clung onto the stone, and the rocks

displayed varieties of reds, pinks, and oranges with white stripes running the span of the cliff side.

The layered colors within the stone were based on the specific order of mineral deposits from an ancient lake: iron giving birth to the red, oranges, and pink pigments, and the white being a purer limestone.

The thick sheets of color stayed level with each other even when separated from hoodoo to hoodoo or by wide gaps between sections that had eroded away at different speeds through time. All of the pieces of this mysterious puzzle were in action, from the earth to the sky, in the variation of colors and the stages of the erosion process visible from the top of the plateau to the canyon floor. It was absolutely amazing.

We continued to walk down the trail with the spectacles of nature enchanting us with every step we took. Soon, we stumbled across a log that was neatly tucked into a bluff, creating a natural awning that provided a place to hide from the sun beating down on us. It was a good place to eat a snack, which Marisa in particular loved to do about every two hours, so we unloaded our sandwiches and chips.

With humans roaming these trails year-round, the wildlife had caught on to the idea that if they did cute little animal tricks, they would be rewarded with scraps.

We encountered many chipmunks, or what we thought to be chipmunks, since the golden-mantled ground squirrels of southern Utah looked like identical twins to their chipmunk brethren from where we were from. They seemed very interested in us, though they may have only been interested in our food.

One little fellow walked within a foot of me, doing cute little things with its paws and cocking its head from left to right, letting me take extreme close-up pictures of him. The little guy won my heart, but I had to stick to my guns, and I did not reward him with any food.

I still kind of feel bad to this day, but he was better off refining his gathering skills than being dependent on humans. I did not believe they put up the "Do Not Feed the Wildlife" signs just to be cruel, but to let nature take its course in the purest fashion without human intervention.

Still, I should have given him something. I feel like I failed to tip a street performer.

Rehydrated and refueled, we continued to follow the yellow brick road through the Land of Oz. The path cut through tight, narrow sections with towering walls on either side. And where one might have been completely stopped by an impenetrable wall of stone, there were small archways carved through the rock to duck through.

After the trail looped around the scenic flats of the land, it turned back towards the canyon's edge. The pathway eventually led to a region known as Wall Street, a deep crevasse cut in the earth. Marisa compared it to the canyons that lead to Petra in Jordan.

"I'm having flashbacks of the Middle East," Marisa stated. "This is so similar to some of the eerie formations spread across the deserts there."

My only comparison was *Indiana Jones*, and my lack of any actual cultural experiences reared its ugly head once again. At least I was on my way to encountering the world on my own terms and beginning to build a list I could reflect back on.

There was a tree that, against all odds, had grown to its full height directly in the middle of the seventy-foot gap between the two monstrous walls of earth that framed the canyon. The tree could not possibly have absorbed the sun's rays for more than a few short hours a day. It reminded me of the small tree on the rock in Yellowstone Lake. Nature had one again found a way to thrive in such a narrow window of opportunity.

Wall Street was the last attraction on Queen's Garden Trail, which immediately began to climb back up the canyon's wall to Sunset Point.

The trail leading the way down the canyon's edge back at Sunrise Point had long sweeping curves that gracefully made their way to the canyon's floor. The path leading back up was a series of sharply inclined short zig zags with stairs at every corner. It felt like climbing the Sears Tower's emergency stairwell in the direct heat of the sun. It just kept going up.

Sweat was pouring out of us as we climbed higher and higher under the sun's relentless rays. Marisa and I drank the remnants of the water we had left. I slowly whispered, "Water ... is ... life," as she drank the last drop.

People were now everywhere, all clogged up by this stairway from hell. We realized that the previous seclusion we had from any other hikers was due to this congested climb.

If you ever find yourself in Bryce Canyon, and I strongly suggest that you go, please note that you should start your hike at Sunset Point. Never make it your exit out of the trail system, especially after a long day of hiking in the sun. That stairway beat us up pretty good.

I would say I am moderately in shape, even though I have not worked out since my eighth-grade gym class—that I flunked—and I have an occasional cigarette (a disgusting habit that I am trying to quit). But as we ascended, I promised myself that this would be the first and last time I ever scaled those stairs to Sunset Point.

Once we reached the top, we were presented with a spectacular view of the terrain we had just traversed. A hoodoo called Thor's Hammer was off in the distance, and we could just make out the small traces of the winding paths we had taken.

We stood there for some time collecting ourselves from the climb. It was well worth it, but we now had to walk the Rim Trail back to our motorcycle.

The Rim Trail, as the name suggests, runs parallel to the edge of the canyon's rim and was a nice, level concrete sidewalk with intimate views overlooking the canyon.

We strolled along, leisurely taking our time and enjoying the scenery until we got back to the bike. We had parked right outside a restaurant/gift store, and we went in to replenish our water supply and snacks.

The afternoon had drained a lot of energy from us, and with Marisa being a big advocate of naps, we headed back to the tipi for some rest. I usually make fun of Marisa and her midday naps, but I was completely on board for getting out of the sun and laying down for an hour or two.

We pulled into our site and noticed the tipi to our right was now occupied, while the girls to our left must have been out exploring the canyons. A man in his thirties was reading a book on a folding chair in the newly inhabited tipi.

We exchanged waves as I disappeared into our tipi for much-needed rest. Marisa zonked out in minutes; I laid there reflecting on the day so far but followed her into the darkness of sleep only moments later.

We woke up an hour or so later with daylight still in the sky and feeling up to the task of another adventure into the canyon. I stepped outside the tipi and introduced myself to our new neighbor.

He and his wife were staying there for a couple of nights before heading back home to California. During our conversation, he mentioned that there was going to be an astronomy presentation with a bunch of telescopes at the main amphitheater just inside the park.

The man explained that they were going to have big, fancy, high-grade telescopes, temporarily loaned by the University of Utah, and amateur hobbyists with their more astronomy-on-a-budget telescopes as well. With all of my previous research about Bryce, I was surprised I had not stumbled across those details on my own.

I thanked him for the information and went to tell Marisa the newly-discovered plan for the night.

"Wanna get lost in the night sky with me tonight?" I asked.

"Um, hell yeah," Marisa shot back without question.

"You want me to explain a little more?"

"You can if you want, but I kinda like the mystery. I'm in regardless," she replied.

We had hours to burn until the event started at ten o'clock, so we decided to wash the filth from our bodies that had collected over the day's hike and do a load of laundry while we had the chance. I jumped in and out of the showers, then manned the washing machine while reading brochures about the park.

I walked around to the back of the laundromat to smoke and ran into one of the clerks that worked in the store connected to the laundromat. He looked just like a thirty-five-year-old Ethan Hawke.

We talked long and in depth about where we came from, what we expected out of life, and what we were doing to achieve those goals. It was a conversation I would have had with real good friends over beers on a Friday night, so I was enjoying the volleying of dialogue with this complete stranger.

It turned out that this man and his wife had saved up money for some time and had bought a small camper to hitch to their old pickup truck.

"We sold everything we had, quit our jobs, and hit the road," he explained. "Now we just ride from one National Park to the next."

"How much money did you start off with, if you don't mind me asking? I mean, how are you able to keep going?" I questioned.

"Well, we saved up a couple years for a foundation of ten grand, and we now pick up temporary jobs within the parks to cover our basic needs, but nothing more. They don't pay us very much, but they cover the pull-in campsite's costs, and the food is discounted, so we just save up for gas money to get to the next leg of the journey."

With a little effort, they had arranged a string of temporary employment from one National Park to another. They still had their emergency fund of around ten thousand dollars, but some of that had been spent on replacing the transmission of their truck. But no matter what the circumstance, they just kept pushing forward.

"That's fantastic!" I said. "My fiancée and I really enjoy exploring around on our motorcycle, and are pretty inspired to do more of it, like, a lot more of it. So your story is hitting pretty close to home."

"Well, letting loose of everything was the best decision we ever made, man," he confidently stated. "It's doesn't have to be just a dream, you know."

It was so close to my dream it was frightening. And here was the living proof that it could be done. Save, sell, and ride. It was that easy. It motivated and energized my soul knowing Marisa and I could possibly do it. Although she wasn't aware that I was having these thoughts, the ideas just started hitting me full force.

This man had completely let go of all possessions and had no home base to retreat back to. That was scary for me, but his story was changing what I thought was possible, and what could actually be done.

Our plan was, if this trip was a success, to have excursions out into the world and then go back home to regather our strength and funds, before launching ourselves back into the wilds again. Maybe never owning, but renting a house, always having somewhere to call home.

We had larger dreams that involved touring across the countless countries Marisa had been to and knew so well. But those were more of the far-fetched dreams that accumulated from the daily grind of our robotic and mundane work routines. But what if we ditched everything, packed up the bike, and hit the road on a limitless journey?

My whole perspective of what could be done was changing over the timespan of two cigarettes. Playing it safe as originally conceived could be viewed as intelligence, or as a weakness, depending on your outlook of risk versus reward.

The conversation with "Mr. Hawke" ignited ideas that bounced around my head like bumper cars for the rest of the day. It was great to meet someone firsthand who broke the mold of the everyday working-class citizen and was able to live his version of the American dream.

He had to return to work, and I had to swap out our clothes from the washer to the dryer. We went our different directions in life, but I now had new-found respect and appreciation for the possibilities in the world. I would continue to dream without fear.

I was back at the tipi folding our clothes and daydreaming about life when Marisa walked in. I excitedly told her about the conversation I had while she had been showering and she sat down on the air mattress, digesting it all.

She explained that there were some possibilities for long term stints, but we had cats, families, and friends that would be hard to walk away from. We decided that we weren't yet sure if full-time adventuring would be the road we wanted to go down, but the idea had been introduced as a possibility.

We started a fire while we waited for the sun to set completely before heading into the canyon for the viewing of the night sky. We left around nine because we didn't know exactly where we were going and wanted to be sure we did not miss anything.

Riding on that road at night was scary. My high beam was blaring in front of us, but beyond the reaches of the headlight was a solid void of complete darkness.

I rode slowly through the twists and turns that led to the parking lot where we were waved in like a landing plane by a police officer with light wands. From there, it was a short walk up a hill to another parking lot, completely surrounded by a black barrier tarp wall to block any light from traffic passing by.

We had arrived just a little too early for them to start letting people in. They were still setting up some of the larger equipment, but said an oral presentation was taking place farther up the hill. So we walked through a campground road to a smaller amphitheater to find the presentation already taking place.

It was very informative, and the instructor added jokes that were aimed at the youth in the crowd. The "Dark Ranger," as he called himself, went on to explain the importance of resisting light pollution because our night skies were being taken from us along with all of their spectacular, observable wonders.

He explained that Rainbow Point in Bryce Canyon was the darkest place in the lower forty-eight states that could be accessed by a paved road. That made it one of the best accessible places to view the night sky with the naked eye or with the assistance of a telescope.

We were just north of that point in what the ranger referred to as one of the last grand sanctuaries of natural darkness. Marisa and I realized at that moment that we wanted to become strong supporters of sanctuaries of natural darkness and should do everything we could to protect them.

We left feeling more intelligent than before the presentation, and walked back down the path to the parking lot where the main attraction would be held. The ranger told us to let our eyes adjust to the darkness for twenty minutes by turning off flashlights and cell phones.

That task was harder than expected as cars now filled up the parking lot. Parents and children were turning their headlights on and driving past us. All of the cars' headlights cancelled out any preparation for our eyes to adapt.

But by the time we reached the main attraction, the heavens above were in full force. We could see the Milky Way from horizon to horizon, and shooting stars darting across the sky. We could point out Mars and Venus with the naked eye, and dozens of constellations, all before we reached the first telescope.

Inside the tarp barriers, there was a big area filled with telescopes, possibly fifty varying in size and cost.

Some were programmable. Type in the coordinates or a predetermined location and it automatically aligned to the star cluster or planet chosen. Others required manually searching for targets by playing connect the dots from landmark stars to the star or planet of interest.

A major rule was not to touch the telescopes under any circumstance. Touching the telescopes would change the focus that had been painstakingly pinpointed.

I was much better at not touching anything than Marisa. If we had been at a strip club, Marisa would have been escorted out.

There was one big mama-jama telescope that people lined up to see like it was the most popular ride at an amusement park. We figured we would start small and work our way to the giant beast of a telescope.

We went from one station to the next, viewing Jupiter, Saturn with its rings, galaxies with weird names like MGC1 and NGC147, and our closest neighboring galaxy with a more familiar name: Andromeda.

The owners of the telescopes really liked to explain everything they knew regarding star clusters and galaxies, describing how dual suns spiraled together to eventually consume each other. It was a lot to take in for someone whose knowledge on the topic came from *Through the Wormhole* with Morgan Freeman, *The Universe*, and other shows that briefly skimmed the surface of what these astronomers discussed in fine detail with other intellectuals on a daily basis over coffee.

I absorbed as much as I could, and deflected some of the information that was way too advanced for me at that point in my understanding.

"Did you know the largest star ever discovered is called UY Scuti, a huge red supergiant that is located 9,500 light-years away in … ma'am, please don't touch the telescope."

"Oops, sorry," Marisa apologized, removing her hand.

"Anyway," the telescope owner continued, "it is located in the Scutum constellation. The star is more than 1,700 times larger than our sun. Ma'am … please refrain—"

"Oh yeah, sorry," Marisa said, backing away. Under her breath she whispered, "I think I totally knocked it out of whack. I can't see anything now."

We continued to look through the eyeholes of different expensive telescopes to see little fuzzy dots that represented star nurseries and globular star clusters. Other dots were dwarf stars some unimaginable miles away from where we stood with different colors representing the gases they burned. All in all, it was pretty amazing stuff.

We never made it to Big Bessie. We stood in line for ten minutes for the monstrous telescope, not really moving, and as much of a reward as it would have been to peer through the big one, I just did not want to wait in a line for that long. I was sure we missed out on something unique that will be hard to stumble across again, but our energy had dwindled down to emergency reserve.

Of all the telescopes we looked through that night, my favorite was the very first one. It was a telescope that cost around seventy-five dollars and was operated by a ten-year-old boy who aimed it at Saturn.

It was the first time I had ever seen the rings of Saturn using my own eye with a little help of polished bent glass. The rings may not have had the same detail as the more expensive telescopes, but you could see them gently curving around the planet. Beautiful.

It left the largest impression on me of the night, and made me think that under the right conditions, I could look up to heavenly bodies on any given night for a small investment of seventy-five bucks and see incredible wonders.

It was getting to be pretty late, and even with the short nap earlier in the day, we were quite fatigued. We decided to walk back to the KTM and call it a night. A very successful night.

Once back at the tipi, we again reflected on the day and the days prior. We were both so astounded by all the things happening around us, and what little it took to explore and to be inspired. It all just added fuel to the fire of traveling more, aiming for the proverbial stars while still taking the time to stop and stare at the ones above.

Chapter 12 - Roads to Remember

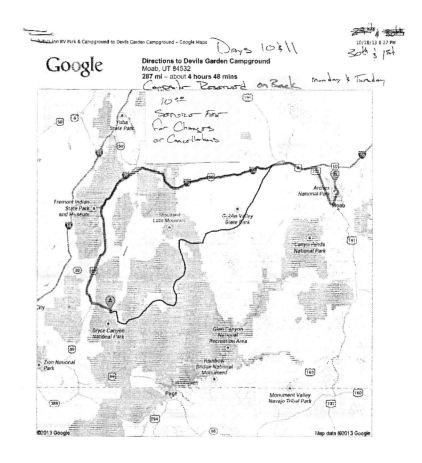

It was sad knowing we were about to leave Bryce Canyon. We could have stayed there much longer. I imagine the two of us will be going back one day to explore it at length and in the finer detail it deserves.

We set to our morning tasks of making coffee, tea, and breakfast as our neighbors began to rouse outside their tipi as well. I went over to say goodbye, exchange pleasantries, and to wish them luck on their trip.

"It was awesome meeting you ladies," I said.

"We wish you two nothing but the best. You guys make an amazing couple," Heather responded. "We're going to pack up and head off to Arches National Park, and then we'll be on our way as well—"

"Really? How did that not come up the other night? That's our next stop too!" I said shocked.

"Ha, well it looks like you're not rid of us yet!" she said excitedly. "We all just woke up, so we're not going anywhere for a long while. But we should exchange numbers so we can meet back up."

"I'll put it in my phone," Marisa chimed in behind me.

"Awesome!" She smiled, whipping out her phone. "We're going to take UT-12 to Escalante and drive through Capital Reef. Someone mentioned it's an amazing scenic drive," she explained.

The route that I had chosen months ago, laying in my bed at home on my computer, took us back to US-89 N then to US-70 E. Their suggestion certainly trumped my previously determined route of pure highway.

I bid them a temporary goodbye and looked at the map from our itinerary packet. It did not mark UT-12. Luckily, there was nothing complicated about our new route: we would take UT-12 and cut through Escalante to UT-24, just as our friends had stated. Once on UT-24, we would then ride through Capitol Reef National Park following it northeast until intersecting with I-70.

The revised route would dramatically cut the amount of highway miles down to a minimum, and when entered on my phone's GPS, it only added thirteen minutes to the original plan. We were thrilled.

Thank the good Lord for word of mouth. The day turned from all highway miles, to riding through another National Park to check off our list. With new excitement flowing through our veins, we loaded the bike up and set off in the direction of Escalante.

The last-minute changes proved the theory that planning loosely and being open to alternative suggestions can lead to excellent opportunities. What we encountered on the way to Arches was an epic adventure within the larger one.

The roads began to wind and weave through the familiar multicolored staircase structures of Bryce. Red and orange rocks protruded out of the earth while the road delicately found the path of least resistance.

We started to follow the bottom edge of a huge colorful cliff to our left, and a forest to our right with more kaleidoscopic bluffs far off in the distance. It was turning out to be the perfect day with some of the best sights we had seen on the whole trip.

Marisa was trigger-happy with the camera once again, capturing the majestic beauty that we were engulfed in. It was while riding down this road that Marisa and I were convinced that we would someday return to Utah, if not move there entirely.

As the road intersected with small towns, I pictured myself in a tiny shack along one of the "main" streets in a residential area with a population of no more than one hundred people. All we would need to live would be one car, my KTM, a small residence, at least two cats, and the grandness of nature surrounding us for hundreds of miles in every direction.

I was daydreaming and driving.

The colors of our surroundings would periodically fade from the reds and oranges to flat greys and blacks, barren of any color. Then the cliffs would burst back to life with all the colors of autumn leaves.

Every once in a while, the road would turn directly into a giant cluster of rocks, cutting right through the walls of the bluff. There were countless little gravel side roads branching off into who-knows-where, and I had to fight the urge not to follow them.

This wonderful road was a visual summary of all the places we had been to so far. We rode through what seemed to be the Badlands on steroids, huge grey mounds of earth that went on for miles. We climbed the sides of sweeping hills tucking in and out of the forest much like the Black Hills. Lastly, we rode on a long straightaway engulfed by bluffs representing all the colors you could imagine. It was the motorcycle trail equivalent of Queen's Garden Loop in Bryce: hoodoos and natural chimneys popping up all around us.

It was a fantastic road. UT-12 should be on the top ten list of everyone's roads to ride, and we had not even ridden halfway through its length between Bryce and Capitol Reef on the map.

After an hour of nothing but eye-opening landscape with stunning rock formations, the land tamed down and became level and flat, but only momentarily.

The short distances of flat terrain between jaw-dropping views were only to reboot all of our senses and prepare us to then be submerged into the new landscape. This magic happened just after the town of Escalante and carried on until UT-12 dead-ended at UT-24.

"I can't imagine the effort it took to build this road," I said over the intercom.

"No kidding. A big thanks to all the unknown people who hacked away at all of this stone," Marisa replied.

"All that hard work so we can lazily ride through on a motorcycle in fascination," I said.

The road was now tightly tucked between two walls of rainbowed earth and eventually led to a pull-off with a view from the heavens. (37.772820, -111.422015) It looked down onto a house nestled into a small section of level ground squeezed between the bluffs surrounding it. We could see the road we were on lead down to the ranch and then continued to snake off into the distance.

While we stood there talking about how insanely awesome the scenery had been so far, our four female friends parked beside us on the pull-off. We all greeted each other as if we had been separated for days.

Marisa and I took pictures of the girls on their camera, and they returned the favor by taking pictures of us standing on the stone ledge barrier with a most spectacular background.

Now that we were all grouped together, Marisa and I started off down the road with the girls following behind us.

There were no dull moments on this road; I cannot express this enough. It was the best road we had traveled down, and we had no original intentions of even going down it. Missing that road would have been the worst unknown thing that could have happened to us.

After what seemed to be riding through the center of the Grand Canyon, the land became grassy and hilly, as opposed to the rocky bluffs we had been riding through. There were sporadic farms in the distance with long gravel driveways leading to the ranches that had likely been there since the mid-1800s.

We soon realized that the cattle and other livestock were definitely free-range. There were a couple of times that I had to come to a complete stop or slow down to five miles an hour to pass and maneuver around wandering cattle in the middle of the road. A flashback to the bison I almost hit in Yellowstone entered my mind, and I let off the throttle around every corner and kept my eyes focused in front of us instead of on the scenery around me.

We came to another pull-off at the crest of one of the larger hills. The ladies followed in behind us, and we took a water break to absorb the new views. (38.011671, -111.358706)

The green hills we had been riding through sloped down into a valley filled with flowers and tall grasses. From our current vantage point, we could see that the hills we were standing on bled back into the ground with the vegetation and trees slowly retreating, giving way to the colorful rocky bluffs we had spent the majority of the day traveling through.

We pressed on, and the road continued through rolling forested hills until the environment changed for the tenth time that day. Just before reaching UT-24, Capitol Reef National Park appeared in all its grandness.

Its towering walls were of a deep red, three times as high as any we had encountered. Once we merged onto UT-24, the road was a front row seat to the greatest show on earth. I just couldn't believe we had almost missed this.

There was no entrance to Capitol Reef National Park, at least not one that we came across. It was just a scenic byway that passed through the heart of some of the most interesting scenery on the planet.

It looked like it could have been the landscape of Mars; it was not of this world. The road began to follow the Fremont River that had already cut a path through the earth, making it an easy place to lay asphalt. The river added pleasant sounds to the overall surrealness of the unimaginable sights passing by.

There were yet again little roads jetting off into the madness that I desperately fought back the urge to wander down. There were pull-offs that led to trails we could have explored for hours.

We did end up pulling into one of the pull-offs to find a pair of coin-operated binoculars pointed at the cliff's side. Thinking it was a strange place for these viewfinders to reside, I peered through, scanning the walls.

"Oh my God, look at that," I said in surprise.

"What do you see?" Marisa asked.

"There are little drawings in the rock," I replied.

"Let me see," she said as she pushed me aside. "Awesome! They're petroglyphs, probably from the Native Americans who lived here."

"Yup, here's a little plaque that states just that." I pointed at it and started reading the short explanation written there. "The carvings in the rock represent local wildlife and inhabitants, and they were made by an ancestral people from the Fremont culture."

I looked back up at the petroglyphs. The torsos of the "human" bodies were downward facing triangles with square blocks representing heads. Out of the squares had antenna-like lines that must have been headdresses, they had stick figure legs, with arms and fingers protruding from the triangular torsos.

"They look more like Rosie the Robot from *The Jetsons* than any human I ever attempted to draw," I said as I looked through the viewport. "Danger, Will Robinson," was echoing in my head.

Any conspiracy theorist would have been convinced aliens landed at that exact spot and wanted their presence to be known to mankind.

I noticed we had unwillingly managed to lose our female companions, and we were traveling by ourselves once again. We got back on the bike and continued down the road following the river with a canopy of trees overhead, and the most beautiful cliffs towering to what seemed to be miles into the sky.

Every time I thought I had seen the most amazing thing in my entire life, something else would pop out and take my breath away.

Once we successfully rode through Capitol Reef, the Martian terrain changed into a lunar landscape. The colors disappeared again, and giant UFO disks sunken halfway into the earth at forty-five-degree angles appeared every hundred feet.

We were on a private rocket of an interstellar tour through an unknown galaxy. Marisa and I rode through Mars, the Moon, and exotic utopias with grins stretched across our faces, barely saying anything because no words could properly describe what we were experiencing.

All at once, the explosion of the temperate terrain settled down to flat, barren desert in place of towering structures and rock formations. Red rocks still scattered the earth, but now only in pebbles with the rare boulder laying around seemingly out of place.

We were on a straightaway that land-speed records could have been broken on. A dry, level road that stretched to the horizon. The fluctuation in the earth's crust within only a few hundred miles went from one extreme to another, then immediately reverted back to the first extremity.

I kept looking down at the temperature gauge on the dashboard of my bike. Marisa and I were fully aware of the heat, but the gauge rose a degree every minute or so. When I had first looked down, it reflected ninety-eight degrees, and over the course of ten minutes we were shocked that it had already risen to one hundred and eight degrees as we rode through the midday sun. The temperature may have only been one hundred and eight, but it felt like a heat index of a million degrees.

"I'm going to pass out from heat stroke," I said over-dramatically.

"So, what am I supposed to do if you pass out?" Marisa asked.

"Hold on tight, and lean in whatever direction you want to steer us until we are going slow enough to bail," I replied.

"That sounds awful. Let's pull over and drink some water," she insisted.

"We're almost there. I'll make it, at least to the next gas station where we can recharge," I promised.

The land stayed fairly flat while we rode on I-70 East for the short distance we traveled along it. We utilized the highway until we turned south on US-191, which led us all the way to Arches.

About ten miles from the Arches National Park entrance, the ground re-emerged out of the earth and turned back into the familiar bluff structures that shot up across the land.

These cliffs were a different variation of the bluffs from both Bryce and Capitol Reef, a new breed of rocks to stare at in wonder: beet-red walls of stone as tall as skyscrapers, ancient and smoothed over by time.

Then, after the most amazing day we had ever had on the bike, we finally arrived at the entrance to the park we would be staying at for the next two nights.

It was blistering hot as we parked the bike at the Arches Visitor Center and ran in to grab pamphlets and familiarize ourselves with the park. We walked inside the building to find a gift shop, a large map of the surrounding area, and little interactive stations that taught us facts about the different rocks and patterns displayed throughout the park.

There was a small group of people sleeping in the corner of the museum. I found it odd, but did not give it much thought, and most importantly, I realized, there was air conditioning. It felt like a fifty-degree variance from the temperature outside.

After we soaked in the air conditioning for a while, we walked back outside to refill our water bottles and venture on to our campsite. There was a sign by the water spigot stating that there were only two places in the whole park that had running water, this being one of them. The other was in Devil's Garden, where we were camping.

At that time, we did not know how far Devil's Garden was from where we stood. We just knew it was in the park, and we were in the park, so how far could it be?

We jumped on the bike and headed back on the road that weaved through Arches. Immediately after the Visitor Center the road began a direct ascent through another set of sharp switchbacks. It hugged a sheer vertical bluff as it crisscrossed its way to the top of the plateau.

Once we reached the top, we saw what looked to be *The Land Before Time*.

"If a velociraptor runs across the road, I will accept it without question," I said.

We began our way to the opposite side of the park, riding past giant stone shark fins that broke the surface of the earth. We passed rock formations that had eroded in such a way that it left huge boulders balancing a hundred feet in the air atop narrow stems of stone. Enormous wall structures divided the land in no particular order, and grand pillars erected skyward, strangely resembling human characteristics.

"I feel like with a little peyote we could have an entirely different kind of journey," I said as I looked around us.

"I don't think I could handle you on peyote," Marisa replied.

"That looks like a silhouette of a pharaoh over there, and over there is a group of nuns bowing their heads praying in a circle." I pointed at the large structures.

My eyes transformed their shapes into the nearest equivalent of a person, place, or thing my mind could relate to. I could imagine any ancient people looking at these rock formations with complete faith that they directly represented the gods.

Marisa was actively taking panoramic pictures of our new surroundings. The sun was still high in the sky, but at an angle that cast sweeping shadows of the larger stone arrangements across the landscape. Marisa took pictures of our own shadows stretching away, desperately trying to escape the connection they had to us.

We continued to ride down the road as it passed landmark after landmark of natural beauty. Not knowing the campground was so far away, we kept thinking it must be just around the next corner. This theory of it being just around the next bend in the road went on for much longer than we anticipated, but it did not matter while we were presented with such extraordinary sights.

Many of the main attractions of Arches were not more than fifty yards from the road. Then there were also side roads that branched off far into the distance. We passed signs that read "Delicate Arch" pointing down a road on the right, "Double Arch" on another offshoot, "Landscape," "Turret," and "Window Arches" signs pointed in different directions.

This park seemed to be filled with a spectacular grouping of structures, all created by the same processes of erosion, but furnishing completely different formations. And I couldn't wait to dive in and start seeing some of them.

Marisa and I finally reached our campground, checked in at the little booth at the entrance, and rode up the hill to where our campsite awaited.

Devil's Garden Campground consisted of one loop that was basically a paved road through the desert with short driveways for parking. Then the asphalt would immediately transform back into the natural terrain of shrubbery, stone, and sand. Some sites were tucked between boulders that emerged out of the ground. Ours was a flat barren site that had no real boundaries that specified how far back it went. (38.775432, -109.587647)

"Welcome to Bedrock, Wilma," I said.

"Was that a lame Flintstones joke?" Marisa asked.

"Yeah, I'm sorry."

"You're better than that, Tim," she said as she walked away shaking her head and faking disappointment.

"You wanna help me set up the tent?" I asked while unloading the bike.

"I yabba-dabba-DOO!" she spat out her best Fred Flintstone impersonation.

We claimed a level patch of earth where we erected the tent. The exact moment that the tarp was laid down, the tent set up, and the interior filled with our soft luggage and the air mattress, was when it occurred to us that our tent was directly under the sun's unyielding rays of heat in the middle of a desert.

There was not much shade to be found, certainly nothing taller than five feet that also had foliage to produce shade. But we emptied out the tent and dragged the entire ensemble down fifteen feet next to the largest bush on the plot of land. We figured it should provide shade for at least a couple of hours in the morning before the sun's angle overtook its protection.

We felt a little more satisfied with the tent's new location, even though it currently doubled as a greenhouse oven, and we now realized why people were sleeping in the visitor center. Marisa and I figured it was a good time to get out of the direct path of the sun and get something to eat.

Where could we find food and shade in the middle of a desert? At the International House of Pancakes of course. We had been riding all day through the blistering sun and needed some time to sit back and relax while eating real food (in air conditioning).

With there not being any restaurants or general stores in the entire National Park, which is a good thing in my opinion, we had to ride the full length of the park and all the way back out into the town of Moab.

It was certainly not the worst ride to dinner, and we figured by the time we were on our return trip through the park, we could witness the sunset and all of its beauty, casting even more shadows and adding the colors of dusk across the already awe-inspiring landscape.

Going in the opposite direction that we came in gave us a new perspective of each landmark we had seen entering. We even discovered new structures unseen riding north that now emerged on the southbound ride into the town of Moab.

Moab boasted having two National Parks within the same town, because both Arches and Canyonlands lay within its borders. Moab would be a prime location to spend a week or more to fully explore all it has to offer, and we were not the only other people to think so. Once in town, we saw dealerships offering a variety of rentals from Jeeps, ATVs, and dirt bikes to take down the aggressive off-road trails that were spread throughout much of the backcountry.

A spark of excitement entered my head as I imagined us traversing through the middle of some red canyon on a rocky path exploring the heart of the land. Standing on the pegs, letting the bike absorb the uneven ground, staring in the direction of where I needed to go, just willing the bike to obey me as a rooster tail of dust launched from the rear of the bike.

I was staring off at a pretty gnarly road full of ruts and trenches. "See that road over there. Wouldn't it be awesome if we—"

"Don't even think about it, Tim," Marisa interrupted before I could finish.

"But …"

"Remember when I had to save you from your ever-so-dangerous tree crossing?" she asked.

She was right of course. Sometimes my excitement gets the better of me, and I end up in trouble.

The outcome of my stupidity in this off-roading scenario could have been much worse than my attempt to cross a log twenty feet in the air. This was a preliminary expedition, and I did not want to chance it turning into our final expedition because of a few bad decisions.

"Yes, I remember," I confirmed.

We pulled in to IHOP and ate a delicious meal while sitting in the air conditioning discussing the trip up to its current destination over tea and coffee.

We had concluded the Midwest and the plains states were not nearly as interesting in comparison to the West. I know there are beautiful locations spread all across this fine nation of ours, and I will never banish the plains states like a rabid animal, but there are so many more wonders grouped in the same area of the western United States.

We wanted to see more. Marisa and I had become infected by the disease of adventure. And for the first time, we felt like this was much more than an annoying itch, but was becoming a basic need that we could no longer live without.

"I want to have more experiences like this," Marisa told me while sipping on her tea. "I want to see more of all the beauty in this world."

I assured her that with enough effort, I believed anything was possible, but we just had to shoot for it. The concrete didn't even have to have fully set before we could walk onto new paths in life. "Even if you don't have the biggest gun on the market, or the most expensive ammo, you can still hit the mark," I said. "We can find a way."

After our relaxing meal and conversation, we headed back to the campsite. Entering and exiting Arches would never get old. It would always be just as amazing as the first time. There would be no chasing the dragon after the initial high. It was now and forevermore the best seventeen-and-a-half-mile pilgrimage to a temporary home I had ever had.

The setting orb of light in the sky was puppeteering shadows across the land as we hoped it would. A cross between *The Nightmare Before Christmas* and any Clint Eastwood Western was the stage that we now performed on.

But what began as the slow descent of the sun quickly turned into a complete lack of any light. People were now exiting the park in a long procession of cars heading south as we rode north.

Darkly silhouetted cliffs against a slightly less black sky looked like shapes cut out of black construction paper that were then glued onto another piece of black construction paper.

We could tell there were shapes within the scenery, but just by the faint outlined borders of the huge monoliths. And just above the horizon, the stars had come out and made a clear defining line of where the earth stood, and where the heavens began.

We made it back to the campsite too late to purchase firewood from the campground host, so we laid down a blanket on the picnic table with a couple of makeshift pillows of clothes and stared at the sky above for the second night in a row.

We pointed out the planets we knew, the constellations we could make out, and watched shooting star after shooting star bolt across the sky like the finale of the galaxy's Fourth of July.

Someone down the road started to play an acoustic guitar, and played every AC\DC and Metallica song he knew, only using power chords. The instrument filled the beautiful empty skies above with sounds that some would call singing and music, but most would call noise pollution.

We retreated to the confines of our tent for sanctuary from the horrible screeches and twangs that originated just down the road. Somehow our tent, nestled between the shrubbery, did a decent job of blocking the sound.

With no rain fly on for the first time of the trip, we looked through the net on the top of our tent at the many stars above until we faded into the ever-so-welcoming blackness of sleep, faintly serenaded by a twelve-year-old ironically playing, "Back in Black."

Chapter 13 - Wrong Way Round

Marisa and I usually slept in until around nine in the morning before we started to move around the bed, accidentally elbowing each other, until we were both fully awake. But that night, we had our sheets and blankets tightly tucked in against the chill of the night, only to wake up sweating before the sun had fully risen.

Moab had the type of uncomfortable heat that made you feel like you could peel a layer of filth off your face. As we stumbled outside, we found it was actually cooler outside than it was in the tent, although not by much.

Knowing the temperature was only going to escalate from that point on, we headed into Arches to explore as much as we could before the full strength of the sun was exposed. We broke open the map of the park to see what was where and tried to chain some of the main interests together while traveling in the same direction.

Our first stop was Delicate Arch, the familiar still-shot pictured on every standard Utah license plate. It was a short ride to it, and with the wind in our face while on the bike, it actually felt like a cool morning.

After leaving the bike in the parking lot, we made sure we had plenty of water and snacks, and then headed onto the trail leading to Delicate Arch.

Another convenience throughout our trip was that our sissy-bar bag converted into a backpack with the removal of two internal straps. It was an excellent way for carrying small loads, both on the bike or while hiking.

I had made the luggage rack/sissy bar combo from a stainless-steel grate used for grilling and a hose hanger that you would mount to a wall. Along with a couple of spacers and a block of wood wrapped in black pleather as a backrest, it turned out to be a pretty nice investment for a total of twelve dollars.

It was my first real farkle on the bike, and you would have thought I paid a hundred and fifty bucks for it. You simply cannot find anything that screws or bolts onto a motorcycle for under a hundred and fifty bucks. Once you add the word motorcycle to anything found online, the price triples.

As we headed down the main trail with our backpack full of goods, we realized that Delicate Arch was not an attraction that was just off the main road. This was a hike well inside the park. The cement trail transformed into a footpath of solid rock that had small indentations from the thousands of people who walked on it. There were man-made trail markers of stacked stones when the trail became less obvious, and you would sometimes have to scan the landscape to find the next little pillar of stones before continuing on. After about forty-five minutes of hiking we came to the top of a large stone hill and saw Delicate Arch in the distance. I scanned the ground for the trail markers with no luck, but the arch was two hundred yards in front of us. So we both figured we would just walk towards it.

What was puzzling us was the fact that the arch was located next to a steep sandstone cliff on one side, and a large bowl-like depression sinking into the earth on the other. We walked to the edge of the bowl and quickly realized that the sides were unclimbable; it was a giant steep crater in the earth.

"What the hell do we do now?" I asked aloud.

There was a lady walking around behind us trying to figure out her next move as well, and we all collaborated to break the mystery.

"My husband climbed that narrow ledge over there on the lip of the bowl," she said as she pointed to the side of a large wall that wrapped around the bowl.

A barely visible, foot-wide ledge eventually led to the flat plateau in the distance. We could see tourists casually walking and standing around safely at the base of the arch.

"He stranded me here to figure out how to get there on my own. Who does that?" the woman said, visibly upset.

"Alright. We have a cliffhanger walk the plank of death to our left, or a shimmy along the intimidatingly steep sandstone cliff to the right that will most likely end up with a helicopter ride to the nearest hospital," I stated.

I couldn't grasp how the average person or small child made it to the arch via either of our two options. But of the two, the sloped sandstone to the right looked to be the safer bet.

We started to climb very slowly, with our chests pressed firmly against the stone. I was not feeling a hundred percent confident that this was the correct way of getting to the arch. In fact, I knew that we were now the equivalent of the two teenage boys in Bryce sliding down the sides of the canyon. People were most likely looking at us in disbelief.

There were holes in the sandstone that I could jam my fingers into for support, but with me in the lead, I only imagined scorpions and spiders lurking within, ready to pounce at my fingertips. And with any swift retreating action of my hand, I would find myself off balance and tumbling down the side of the cliff, only to see Marisa's look of terror every full rotation as I spun to my demise.

My knees began to quiver and shake as the sandstone cliff became steeper.

I said, "Hey, guys, you two should turn around right now. This is pure stupidity."

As afraid as I was for myself, I was twice as afraid for Marisa and the stranger we convinced to follow us like a lemming to our deaths. (38.7397026,-109.5003985)

I saw a flat shelf of rock just above me. After a mighty lunge, I pulled myself up onto it and then sat down to collect my nerves. I had a much longer arm span than Marisa and knew she would not be able to pull herself up at this awkward angle.

But once on the shelf, I realized I had gotten to a point of no return. There was no going back down the way I came.

I looked up to see I was only a good twenty feet or so from the flat plateau above. I was, however, sitting on a shelf with a most spectacular view of the arch directly above me that only experienced climbers and complete idiots such as myself had been able to see. I took a photo opportunity to claim my prize of stupidity.

A man walked to the edge of the plateau above and yelled down to the woman following Marisa, "What in the hell are you doing?" The man turned out to be the mystery husband who had ditched the lady following us. Marisa and the man's wife had already retreated back the way they came, but I was now faced with twenty more feet above me until I would safely be planted back on both of my feet.

I am around six feet tall, with a reaching arm span of two feet above my head. The man above, who was patiently waiting to pull me up, had a reaching span of around three feet, so I realistically had to make it another nine or so feet before I could be saved for the umpteenth time in my life from a situation I should have never put myself into.

I had drawn a small crowd that now peered over the edge to watch me slide my way up the vertical sandstone wall. I shook with fear as I slowly progressed upward.

My legs buckled as I tried to lock my feet into small notches in the cliff's edge. The full weight of my body was suspended by only three fingers at times. Distant "ohhs" and "ahhs" came from the whispering crowd above.

Finally, I was able to clasp hands with the husband. With a quick jerk, I was up and freed, now sporting holes in my shirt from scraping against the cliff's edge.

Our full concentration was now on the women who we had both led, in our own way, to a fairly uncomfortable predicament. Thankfully they had made it halfway back to where they had started and were now at the base of the arch where tall natural steps led to the safety of the rest of the tourists.

Marisa fearlessly lunged and pulled herself up each five-foot step and I was finally able to hoist her up to safety. The wife of the man was directly behind Marisa.

Once they were on level, solid ground, the wife slapped her husband screaming, "Don't you ever abandon me like that again!"

Marisa and I just embraced each other, very happy that neither of us fell to our deaths.

We walked to where the population of people gathered, keeping our heads down and not making direct eye contact with anyone out of embarrassment.

At the back of the plateau we found a flat concrete pathway that was six feet wide that led around the opposite side of the massive bowl, clearly a proper trail. On the other side of that same wall was where the husband had crossed on the small lip.

If we had walked back two hundred feet from where we had originally started, we would have found the main trail that led up a concrete stairway. We definitely took the wrong way round.

Marisa and I sat down to drink some water and eat some snacks, both of us very grateful to be safe. After our nerves settled, and we had taken in the view long enough from every angle possible, we started down the newly discovered path that led to the trail system back to the parking lot.

As we walked down the trail, we overheard people talking about three climbers that foolishly almost got stuck on the side of the arch. Word had already spread about us.

We made it back to the bike and agreed we would not put ourselves in any more stupid situations, a hard task to guarantee when traveling with me. We looked at the map and headed to the next set of arches down the road.

Turret Arch and Window Arch were a hundred yards from each other. Window Arch was a gigantic sprawling arch with an open view all the way to the horizon of the desert. We walked directly under the arch and sat down at the base to gaze into the distance.

This would have been a calming and peaceful experience if it wasn't for the overwhelming wind from the open hole in the cliff wall. The gusts were intense and kicked up sand everywhere, creating mini cyclones inside the arch. We looked out toward the landscape until the amount of sand whipping into our eyes and mouths forced us to retreat.

Multiple pathways led around the arch and connected to various trails in a large loop that all reconnected back to Turret Arch. We walked around snapping pictures while taking our time. Our urgency and fast-pace lifestyle had halted, ever since our latest near-death experience just a few hours before. At a leisurely pace while soaking it all in, we eventually made our way to Turret Arch, and then back to the KTM.

The midday heat was now in full force, and I wanted to ride around with the wind blowing in my face, without sand, that is. So we decided to ride out of the park and go to Canyonlands. This would add another National Park to our list, and we had heard great things about what it had to offer.

Once out of Arches, we headed north on US-191 to get to the intersection that led to Canyonlands. As we turned onto UT-313 East, we started to see signs for "Dead Horse Point State Park." Being in no particular hurry to get anywhere, we headed down the road leading to Dead Horse Point.

We arrived at the parking lot of Dead Horse after a short ride through some amazing scenery and twisting roads. Marisa and I walked to the edge of the clifftop balcony overlooking the valley below. She took pictures of the wide canyon with the Colorado River running through the middle of it. We could have posted those pictures online and convinced everyone we had gone to the Grand Canyon. It was as massively wide as it was beautiful.

Marisa read a plaque that described how the park was named. It was a legend that a group of outlaw cowboys had rounded up wild mustangs and herded them to the tip of the canyon's edge. The cowboys made a fence of brush and branches that held the horses in on the face of the corral. The remaining sides were just sheer drops to the canyon floor thousands of feet below. The cowboys then took the mustangs of their choosing, and left the rest pinned in the makeshift corral.

After abandoning the horses for an extended amount of time, the horses could smell the water of the Colorado River below. Out of pure thirst, the horses leapt to their death to the canyon floor.

It was a horribly sad story, and Marisa's love of horses made it even worse for her.

We left the park glad to have gone in and to have learned some of the local folklore. It was an absolutely beautiful place, regardless of the story's authenticity (at least I was hoping it wasn't true). I tried to convince Marisa that there are many landmarks with stupid names, having absolutely nothing to do with anything relevant. Even with my false hope I could still see in her eyes the grief and heartache for the horses who might had died long ago.

We continued onto Canyonlands, and once in the park, Marisa stated she was beginning to get hungry. I saw a gravel road shooting off to the left of the main drive just after the entrance. I told her that I just wanted to see where it led, and we would get something to eat afterwards. It was too tempting not to turn down.

As we rode down the new path, it began to turn from gravel to compacted sand. It was nothing to be too concerned about, but I was sure to take my time and ride as safely as possible.

The road made its way to the edge of a canyon with the grandest view we had seen so far. The view, after the immediate drop to our left, was of canyons, and the flat valleys between them stretching all the way to the horizon. This was Wile E. Coyote and the Road Runner's playground.

As immensely grand the view was just to my left, I was not going to take my eyes off the loose gravel and sand mixture directly in front of me. We continued riding along the twelve-foot-wide path with a stone wall to our right and an immediate drop-off down the entire face of the canyon to our left.

Very quickly, our new private drive became much more extreme than we anticipated. But it was magical.

The path turned out to be one of the trails you would take a dirt bike, ATV, or Jeep on. But we kept going because the views were too outrageous as we cruised along the canyon's edge. We followed a huge, concave bend in the canyon, and could see just how elevated we were based on the height of the same road across the gap of the long sweeping curve.

A pull-off emerged on the left. It was just a flattened section of multiple gigantic stones that jetted out over the canyon ledge. (38.457204, -109.816648)_We stopped to stare in wonder for the millionth time of the trip. This was the first truly off-road back-country experience we had so far, and I was very proud of my bike, as well as myself.

As Marisa and I stood there, three dirt bikes rolled up onto the ledge alongside us.

The three riders were an eccentric group from Arkansas, riding on slightly more appropriate motorcycles for the terrain including the addition of knobby tires. By slightly more appropriate, I mean massively more appropriate given the road we wondered down. They were fully dressed in your typical motocross gear with hydration packs and helmets.

I could not imagine what they must have thought of Marisa and me. We were both in shorts and a T-shirt, with no helmets, casually strolling around sightseeing on our KTM, equipped with nothing but street tires, riding down the same aggressive track as them.

They pointed at a trail directly below us that violently zig-zagged back and forth across the face of the canyon at a very steep angle. They then informed us that the road we were currently riding down turned into that very trail.

We broke out our map of the area and realized we had not turned down a peaceful road leading to some attraction within Canyonlands, but instead, were in the heart of the main attraction via the backroads.

The three riders consisted of a father and son duo, along with a good friend they had met in Utah the year prior, who was also from Arkansas. They had been traveling through the backcountry of Utah, Colorado, and neighboring states on their dirt bikes.

None of them were cocky, even though it was apparent we were not dressed for the occasion and out of place. The drastic comparison between them and ourselves could not have been further apart. Bret, the father and more talkative of the group, did make fun of my leather designer boots, stating they were just too fancy for off-road motorcycling.

"They've served me well so far," I protested. "They take the place of both enduro boots and standard hiking boots."

Space is very precious on a motorcycle; any hybrid footwear would suit you better than needing two pairs for different applications, I reasoned.

Bret didn't care, and called me fancy boots from that point on. It was like we were immediate friends.

As we looked at the map, the trio showed us their intended route. Their only insight of the road conditions ahead was from the previous year, but they stated that if we went slow enough, we would be able to follow them down the zig-zagging canyon face and out into the backcountry.

I let them know right off the bat that this was my first rodeo, and my confidence level was hovering at just above 10 percent due to almost dying just a couple of hours earlier in the day. But at the same time, I was completely 100 percent in for doing it.

We then all looked at Marisa. Marisa looked at the road below, then looked at me and said, "Let's do it," like the champion she was. She then immediately made a follow-up statement by saying that if at any point in time she said to turn around, we would turn around. That was the best response I could had ever hoped for out of her.

I figured we might not ever get another chance to have an escort of experienced riders assist a pair of two-up, first time rookies, wearing shorts, T-shirts, and designer boots down the face of a canyon that rode off into the sunset. It was irresistibly irresponsible, but that seemed to be my life's motto.

We got on the bike, and once I mounted and turned on our little action camera, we followed Zach (Bret's son) and Brian down the face of the canyon, while Bret hung back to film the descent.

We were off and riding along the cliff's edge on a trail built of patches of compact dirt, gravel, and sand. I put on my best impersonation of a knowledgeable off-road riding motorcyclist as the trail started to become more challenging. This was all taking place while every part of me was screaming that I had absolutely no right being there.

Zach stopped to film Brian's descent, who had by then taken a substantial lead ahead of us, but Marisa and I carried on. That is until we got to the very first switchback.

I was not going more than ten miles an hour and using the friction of first gear to slow down to a very manageable speed without using the brakes. As we rounded the first corner, I applied the brakes, but was not able to steer the bike left.

"Oh crap, this is bad!" I said as I started to panic.

I freaked out and hit the brakes in full force only to slide another seven feet before being able to come to a complete stop.

As soon as I was able to stop, Marisa could tell that it had not gone as smoothly as I had anticipated, and quickly dismounted the KTM.

"What's wrong, love?" I asked innocently.

"Really? You basically just screamed we're going to die, then asked what's wrong?"

She said she no longer felt the need to participate in the day's activities. It was then that I realized we were on a hairpin turn on a steep incline in sand. To be completely honest, I was way out of my league, and should not have gone down the black diamond hill so early in my off-roading career.

My awesome decision-making skills had yet again put me in a situation that I was forced to deal with on the fly. It was a trial by fire; there were no emergency exit drills that prepared me for turning around a six-foot-long, five-hundred-pound motorcycle on a steep incline in sand.

But it was as good of a time as any to figure out how to do so.

A four-wheel drive truck had pulled up behind us looking to pass me, and a man yelled out the window, "Do you need to turn around?"

"Sure do," I answered thankfully. "I have no idea how I'm going to do it, but that's the goal."

I killed the engine as he walked down to my bike, and we devised a plan of action. I could ride the KTM in neutral down the hill, turning left sharply until the bike was perpendicular to the road. Then he could push me backwards, turning sharply in the opposite direction, until I reached the very edge of the cliff where I could start the bike and climb back up the hill.

Zach came riding down just in time to witness me shamefully having to turn the bike around. I yelled out to him that Marisa had freaked out and would not let me continue even though my heart was still in the game.

Marisa smirked at me with a look that reflected, "Oh really, is that what happened?"

The newest rescuer in my accident-prone life began the process of turning my bike around. We executed our pre-planned strategy flawlessly. I was just happy I did not drop my bike in the transitions.

Once the nose of the bike was facing the correct direction, I started the engine, and rode up the hill to Zach. I blamed us turning around on Marisa, like strong, confident men do.

I knew the Arkansans were staying in Moab from our previous discussions while parked on the side of the canyon's edge. So although I was going back up the way I came, I gave Zach our campsite number and said they were more than welcome to stop by to share the stories of the road we missed.

With that, Marisa and I wished Zach luck on his journey and he took off down the road. It was then that I realized I had recorded the entire shameful event, so I turned off our not-a-lot-of-action camera.

A short jog up the road we ran into Bret. I extended him the same invitation to our campsite and wished him luck on the rest of his trip in the event we never crossed paths again. He told me to keep my boots shiny, and took off after his son and friend down into the curves that looked so easy to traverse from afar.

Shafer Canyon Road had beaten me the first round, but I had gained a nemesis in Utah that I would train vigorously to conquer on our next bout.

We rode back up the trail, followed the canyon, and retreated to the main road that led to Canyonlands' Visitor Center.

We had started the trend of adding bumper stickers to the bike's panniers back when we were in the Badlands. But while in the gift shop, I did not feel that I had fully earned my Canyonlands badge-of-honor yet. So, I only purchased an Arches sticker to add alongside the Bryce Canyon, Badlands, and Yellowstone stickers.

Marisa's hunger was now beginning to turn her against me and there was no food to be found in Canyonlands. So we left without being able to penetrate deep into the park.

I felt that the little amount of time we did spend in the park had been utilized to its fullest potential, letting me know exactly where I stood in my skillset of off-road riding. We left the park knowing it ranked high on the list of places that would be explored further at a future point in time.

We rode into Moab and ate at a small, privately-owned bakery that doubled as the owner's home. After a good fresh meal, we wanted to continue probing around the area. One of the locals informed us of a scenic road that went into the hilly mountainsides just to the south of Moab.

The gentleman who enlightened us about this loop stated the main road was paved, but there would be many opportunities to go down smaller gravel offshoots. The side roads ranged from fairly easy to very difficult depending on the particular road chosen. I was up for the opportunity of choice, but did not know if I would take any of the paths off the main junction, considering my luck so far that day.

With our map marked with the location of LaSal Loop Drive's entrance, we headed out to find our next improvised point of interest.

Once we found LaSal Loop, we began to climb the side of a gigantic hill that broke the earth up from flat desert plains in the west, to mountains that peaked in the near distance to the east. The road wound along a leading edge overlooking the smaller towns south of Moab.

Marisa began to film and take pictures as the road snaked around the outer edges of the rocky beast of a hill. The road dipped into the forest only to reemerge to the cliffside for a moment, and then back into the forest. It was like going from a hot tub to the cold of a swimming pool, such an explosion of different sensations from the landscape.

We did see many gravel offshoots, and I held out as long as I could until a particular path caught my interest. I looked back at Marisa for approval, and I was at first denied, but was eventually able to convince her to let me throw the bike onto roads that were less than ideal.

The gravel road marked FR0065 started off innocently enough. It was a bit choppy and had plenty of rivets that began to feel like we were on a broken washing machine in its spin cycle. It was not nearly as threatening as Shafer Canyon Road, and there was no sand on its surface. (38.5471962,-109.2921327)

What it did have were small waterfalls popping out of the rock walls to our side, all collecting into a river busily making its way back down the mountain. The trees, fresh water, and clean air pushed us onward.

But then the road morphed into sharp "S" curves that sliced up the steeper terrain filled with loose gravel. It started to become more and more intimidating. Marisa finally said we had gone far enough, but I wanted to push on a little farther.

Going uphill always seemed to be easier for me than fighting the force of gravity on loose roads that continually tried to pull me and the bike down to the ground. But every successful gravel hairpin turn I completed on the sharp incline added another obstacle to the return trip down. It was both exhilarating as well as nerve-wracking. I was climbing and riding fairly comfortably, trying to shake off some of the shame from the defeat earlier in the day.

We rounded an extremely sharp turn ending up on a steep incline of loose rock, sandwiched between a hill to our right, and an immediate drop-off to our left. It was not the end of the line, but I knew the road had been breached far enough. I killed the engine, parked the bike on the flattest portion of the road, and we dismounted the motorcycle.

The crashing of water from a distant waterfall, and a view that seemed to be out of a tropical rainforest were our newest surroundings. I felt satisfied with my beginner off-road course that did not over-intimidate me to the point of turning around prematurely. It was a small victory for my ego, since I did not have a very long winning streak from the paths I had chosen throughout the day.

After I turned the motorcycle around, we started to make our way down the sharp curves of the gravel roadway. I was able to coast in neutral for the majority of the way down, only applying the brakes around the sharp corners.

I had finally ridden into a trail system, rode a healthy portion up steep hills on questionable terrain, and successfully made it back without dropping the bike, losing my nerves, or having Marisa jump off to start hiking back on foot. It was a good feeling and hopefully the first of many to come.

We continued our way around the loop until we arrived at a pull-off overlooking what looked like Monument Valley on a smaller scale. We pulled over and sat down to reflect on the day so far and looked out toward the newest awe that was spread before us.

There were so many attractions we could get lost in for days, it made us never want to go back home, if it wasn't for our cats of course. I missed those little guys more and more every day.

We again found ourselves talking about how we could manage to cut loose for a potential extended amount of time. The daily commute to and from work, with spotted days off over the period of an entire year, just didn't sound like enough.

"How much money do you think we would need to take off for three years?" Marisa asked.

"I have no idea, but there are plenty of resources online from people who have," I replied.

"We should look into that," she said.

"We should definitely look into that," I confirmed.

The sun was setting, making the landscape appear redder than ever. We knew this last stretch of the drive back to Arches was going to be amazing.

We pushed forward down the road until it finally came to its end as it intersected with UT-128. We turned left, and ran directly into the mighty Colorado River that cut a canyon into the plateau. We followed UT-128 as it snaked its way around the eastern edge of the river with amazing bluffs on either side.

After navigating next to the river for a few miles, we saw a boat launch with a small beach. We pulled into the beach area just as the sun was beginning to make its way back down toward the horizon.

We sat on the river's edge, looking at the canyon wall across the water at what I imagined to be huge ancient Egyptian paintings on the rock face. (38.663135, -109.500198)

Contrasting stretches of black stone and shadows created tall human silhouettes. They stood with staffs to their sides, each wearing different animal headdresses representing their different gods. It was a bit like finding shapes in the clouds, but if you looked hard enough, you could find just about anything. I saw ancient Egyptians. If they were an inkblot test, I don't know what conclusions could be drawn about my personality.

Wanting to get back to the campsite before the sun was completely down, we started riding back alongside the river until we hit US-191, just south of Arches. We then began our ascent back up the switchbacks at the entrance of the park and continued into Arches while the sun steadily dropped.

As we rode past the parking lot of Balance Rock, I saw a small boy pick up something small off the ground, and then launch it in a perfect rainbow into the road ahead of me. I heard a loud *dink, blop, plow*. The kid had made a direct hit and sunk my battleship.

I am fairly sure he did not specifically try to hit me with a pebble, that would have involved some on-the-spot quick calculating and math prior to the launch of the stone, but I was pissed nonetheless.

"That little bastard!" I said over the intercom.

"What are you swearing about now?" Marisa asked, not seeing or hearing what I had just witnessed.

"Some little kid just chucked a rock at us," I said.

I slowed down and turned my head to see the parents already taking corrective actions, but I still gave the universal sign of displeasure with a middle finger.

I could have stopped to inspect for damage but did not see an outcome where I would actually ride back demanding money from the tourist. I just hoped there wasn't any noticeable damage and continued on to our campsite.

When we finally pulled into the campground entrance, to our complete and utter surprise, there stood Bret, Zach, Brian, and another dirt-biking companion of theirs, Fletcher. The invitation to our campsite was honest and sincere, but I did not expect that I would ever see any of them again. It was one of those things you kindly say to people, but never think they would actually follow through with.

I could not have been happier that they did. We all parked our bikes at my campsite and began telling stories of the who, what, where, why, and when that had all led us to where we now stood.

Marisa and I had not prepared for guests, so we did not have any beer or firewood. But there was plenty of trail mix, beef jerky, and friendly conversation to go around.

We sat around the picnic table telling jokes and recalling some of the humorous things that happen to travelers, especially to those so exposed to the elements. I told them of our multiple encounters with death, all taking place within that very same day.

In return, they told us about what we had missed on Shafer Canyon Road, and how it may have been best that we turned around when we did. I am not sure if they were trying to mend my ego, but either way, I knew we made an intelligent decision to turn around to fight another day.

The storytelling, which was being passed back and forth between both parties, eventually led up to the small child who had just recently thrown a rock at my bike. I admit I retold the story's details in a slightly more dramatic fashion than what had actually occurred.

"There I was riding along, in tune with nature, without a care in the world. Marisa, the love of my life, was on the back of the bike, peacefully humming The Beatles 'Long and Winding Road.' Then, out of nowhere, appeared a small devil child."

I put the flashlight under my chin so that my face lit up as I continued the story.

"The child's squinted eyes glowed red against the dark backdrop of the night sky. I saw him calculating the wind's direction and speed with a wet index finger, only then to hone in his demon-red eyes on me.

"He then reached down, deciding between different weights, shapes, and sizes of various rocks on the ground, tossing less-quality stones aside. Once he finally chose a projectile that would have the best aerodynamic properties for his evil task, he again evaluated the wind to confirm nothing had changed.

"With my speed and direction of travel estimated, he drew back his frail arm. As tiny as his frame was, the devil within gave him the strength to catapult the stone towards my fragile body.

"I saw space and time bend around the stone, creating a tail much like that of a comet's. I was able to make the slightest adjustment, weaving left out of the direct path of the stone. This prevented certain doom, but in doing so, I had put my trusty steed in the impact zone.

"My KTM groaned in pain and snorted with a loud rev from the engine without me twisting the throttle.

"I looked back to the child, who's eyes were gradually intensifying to supernovas as he chanted, his tongue flickering wildly. Suddenly, what seemed to be a black hole appeared around him, and then collapsed into itself, leaving nothing behind except a burning ember of a piece of coal laying on the ground where he had stood."

Upon the completion of my tale, I pointed to the scar that my bike now wore as proof of the encounter with the demon on the side of the road.

As they gathered around the bike to inspect the damage, flashlights were passed around so that they could see, if they concentrated hard enough, where paint may, or may not have been missing.

I was still pissed, but after the damage had been assessed, and the realization that the only harm done was a small chink of paint scratched off the plastic molding around my gas tank, I was able to laugh it off.

Marisa and I had ridden thousands of miles. We had ridden down trails that I should have never gone down, and I very well could have dropped my bike several times. But through it all, the only damage that my bike had sustained was from a small boy. I accepted that, because it wasn't nearly as bad as it could have played out in multiple different scenarios.

As we sat there laughing about our lives, the sun had almost completely set. Our campsite was on the west side of the campground loop, and the three conjoining sites directly across from ours were occupied by a large group of Hasidic Jews.

We had noticed them throughout the evening without too much attention. At first glance, they seemed slightly out of place, but the more I thought about it, the more I realized that our surroundings were an ideal location for a religious setting. I am not a religious person myself, but I felt closer to nature, and had a warm fuzzy feeling inside while in the middle of such natural beauty.

As the sun began to make its final descent below the horizon, the group of twenty or so Hasidic Jews all faced our campsite, and started chanting in the direction of the setting sun directly behind us. We had front row seats to them singing in unison.

It was a very unique experience, and I am sure it was an intimate moment for them, so we tried our best not to stare. After they finished, they dispersed between the three campsites across from us. It was incredible to witness firsthand.

This was our last night in Utah, and the state had proved to be amazing on multiple levels. But now we knew we had to leave it.

We showed Bret and his friends our itinerary for the next day. We were to ride to Frisco, Colorado the entire way via US-70. Bret and his crew had just come from that direction a few days before and told us about a scenic route to get to Grand Junction. This would take us a little farther south initially, but then we would ride northeast, being presented with exceptional views while riding through the canyons of Gateway, Colorado.

Bret took out his map, and then drew a squiggly line on ours that best represented the route they had taken. Marisa and I agreed that this would be our new route based on everyone's descriptions and excitement.

The sun was now completely down, and our four new companions had a thirty-five-minute ride just to get out of the park. We exchanged some of our personal information, wished each other luck on the journey ahead, and bade each other farewell.

As they rode off into the night, I was very grateful that they had decided to take us up on our invitation to visit our campsite.

Marisa and I were exhausted from the day's activities. It had been full of danger, adventure, beauty, and laughter. We crawled into our tent fully satisfied and called it a night.

As we lay there with our eyes closed, we listened to our neighbors across the road tell an old Jewish legend. The storyteller would accompany his tale with sections of guitar playing and song. It was very pleasant, like a lullaby that slowly eased me into sleep.

Chapter 14 - Gateway to Enlightenment

Marisa and I woke up early once again in order to beat the sun's wrath. The original route for the day would have taken us back to US-70 and added a full day of highway riding all the way to Frisco, Colorado. Luckily, because of word of mouth, we were now armed with a way to avoid much of the highway miles, and would instead be cutting through the heart of the scenery.

As we rode away from Moab's barren landscape, I realized with a tinge of sadness that we had traveled as far west as we would. From here on out, we would only travel eastward.

We still had five days left of our trip, but it felt as if we were already on our way home. This realization hit me hard, because my heart was not yet ready to start traveling home.

I felt as if a timer had been set on a countdown back to our regular life. Regular life. It was like I could hear the constant ticking in my ears.

This trip had proved to be much more than we had anticipated. I had expected it to be fun, and maybe have some breathtaking views, but I didn't expect it to change me so deeply in my core.

Marisa and I had not crossed any remote deserts, nor did we meet any indigenous people in faraway lands, there were no river crossings or border checkpoints, and I can only assume we were always within ten miles from a gas station at any given point in time.

But this trip had fueled a fire that I did not fully understand until we were smack dab in the middle of it all. I was now burning to keep going, to keep heading west until there was no more west to go to, and even then, find a way to continue on. To get on the bike every day with nothing but road ahead of me.

But instead, we were now going east. Back to work, back to our cars with air conditioning and cup holders, back to our daily rhythm of life. It was comfortable and safe at home, that was for sure, but a part of me no longer wanted to go back.

The bummed-out feeling disappeared once we found ourselves immersed back into the grand scenery on the single lane roads that cut through the canyons of Utah.

We were still not accustomed to the wonders of our surroundings, even though we had ridden on very similar roads throughout the trip. We traveled for hours following a river cut deep into the earth to our left, and a canyon wall that was most likely cut by the same river over a millennium ago to our right.

We passed a luxury resort in Gateway, Colorado with Teslas and Maseratis parked within its extravagant gates. This was definitely a wealthy person's playground. The roads had flat and sexy curves that I could imagine floating down at a hundred and eighty miles an hour behind the wheel of a hundred-and-eighty-thousand-dollar automobile.

As we rode along, my mind faded to a purely blissful state of wondering what else was beyond the safety net of America's byways and highways. Marisa had traveled the world at large, and I now internally begged for the chance to experience some of the same wonders.

I pictured us riding through Jordan to see Petra, or in Egypt to see the pyramids, and somewhere lost in Mexico or Argentina. I wanted to get lost on every continent ... actually, I hated getting lost. I wanted to ride triumphantly across every continent (except Antarctica).

Suddenly, I realized that this was my new mission. This was my purpose. It was decided, and all I had to do now was plot how to make it a reality as opposed to just an idea.

As I daydreamt about the future, the surrounding scenery was like classical music playing in the background while reading a good book. I was not one hundred percent paying attention to it as I concentrated on my newly discovered life goals deep within, but the surrounding beauty enhanced and purified my inner mental conversation.

I am not sure how long we followed the road as it delicately sliced through walls of stone and around natural chimneys, but it was as good as any setting to reflect on our life's options.

As we continued to ride through the grandness of nature, I pondered what I had learned so far. Our setup was very amateur, and it would not be suitable for months, let alone years' worth of travel.

Our tent was on the larger size, which we both liked, but was mounted underneath our left pannier in a not-so-ideal location. It was attached with two heavy-duty Velcro straps with D rings that shackled to the frame of the pannier rack. It was then pulled up flush to the bottom of the pannier with three bungees. This set-up left us unable to open the left case without first undoing the bungie nightmare.

There was no other place to strategically attach the tent to the bike. This was due to the odd shape of our only other luggage besides the panniers: the T-Bag that was mounted to my homemade luggage rack/sissy bar.

The bag seemed like a good fit at first, but it was a narrow vertical storage system, not a wide horizontal one. There was only one entry point into the bag via a small horseshoe zipper at the top. We were forced to stack layers on top of each other, with the most important items on top for easy access.

Getting to any needed items at the bottom involved us taking off the sleeping bag, which we strapped down on top of the whole assembly, unzipping the only access point, and then taking out all of the items until we dug far enough to reach the particular item.

This was not the polished setup one envisions when thinking of exploring long distances on a motorcycle. We currently resembled the motorcycle equivalent to the truck in the opening credits of Beverly Hillbillies, and if we were ever going to do some serious adventure riding, we needed to refine our system.

There was also the uncertainty of the blow-up queen air mattress. It was very comfortable when fully inflated, but it had already sprung a leak once, so I was not confident about its durability with constant use.

The bike was also not very well protected; it would need an upgrade to a beefier crash bar exoskeleton for the inevitable cases when it would be laid down. The plastic tank "guards" that came stock would do absolutely nothing if dropped. It also had a plastic skid plate on the bottom that would protect against very little. The same could have been said for the plastic hand guards: one drop and I would have one less hand guard.

The list of farkles could go on as far as, and beyond, what my budget would have allowed. I needed to refine the list down to what was absolutely needed for long distance travel. Weight and space were issues, and they both went hand-in-hand. The more space you had, the more likely you would fill it with things, some of which may never even be used.

So we needed a better packing solution, especially on the rear of the bike where the T-Bag was. But with the addition of a tank bag for smaller, more readily available items, that would hopefully be enough space for our daily—

"Tim, are you even paying attention to what I'm saying?" Marisa asked, breaking through my wall of focused concentration.

"Umm, short answer, no," I replied. "What's up?"

"I'm hungry and want to stretch my legs," she stated through the fuzzy microphone.

Oh yeah, and we would need a better intercom system. Wait a minute, I thought. I didn't even know if Marisa wanted to go on this crazy pipe-dream journey with me ...

I suddenly realized that we were now riding on US-70 and only an hour away from our hotel for the night. We had made it into Colorado, adding to the list for a combined total of six states traversed via the motorcycle.

Red sandstone had turned into jagged granite, and the foothills surrounding us had become increasingly covered in evergreen trees.

We pulled over for a meal and a stretch and found ourselves in the middle of ski resort central. We were surrounded by huge lodges perched on the sides of steep slopes, with the trees cut in perfect lines for ski lifts. Little winding paths had been shaved along the scalp of the forest where, in the peak season, skiers would slalom down through the snow.

The temperature had certainly dropped, and for me, the crisp air was a welcome relief. We had just left the extreme heat and barren landscape of Utah, and the flat land that went on as far as the eye could see was now interrupted by the enormous snow-tipped peaks of the Rockies.

After our short break, we continued to follow the GPS until we arrived at the inn that I had randomly chosen as a stopping point months prior. We parked the bike and walked inside to check in.

With our mode of transportation fairly obvious by our clothing, and after the clerk behind the counter glanced at my Illinois driver's license, he inquired about what we might be up to on a motorcycle in Colorado.

I rattled off our trip up to that point and his eyes lit up. The man excitedly walked with us outside to take a look at our bike. He beamed with excitement as he then led us to the garage connected to the hotel and opened the door to show us his KTM 650 that he rode on all of the local trails.

The man explained that the smaller bike was better for the short stints in and out of the single-track paths that were scattered throughout the surrounding mountain ranges. He loved his 650cc, but he had always longed for a bigger bike, and had specifically been eyeing the 1190 Adventure.

The clerk was from Romania, with dark features and a faded accent. He was not very tall and stated the height of our KTM was intimidating.

"Throw a leg over," I told him.

"Thank you, but I think I'd need a step stool," he replied.

I said, "Well I know it's tall, but it's an awesome bike. Especially for what we plan on putting it through."

"Where exactly are you going?" he asked.

"The world!" I said excitedly.

"The world?" Marisa wondered aloud.

I glanced over at her, unsure how she was going to react to my new life goal and dreams. "Yes, well, you know … we want to go to a lot of places on this bike," I finally stated.

The man's eyes were bright and sizzling. "Too few people have the real possibility of pursuing their dreams," he said. "Even fewer actually set their dreams into motion and follow through on things they lay awake at night wondering about."

I said, "I couldn't agree more. Too many people's lives have become the back and forth motion of working to live, and living to work."

The clerk brought us back inside, taking us on a short tour of his hotel and his life. "My wife and I saved money for years in order to break free of the nine-to-five jobs we both had. But once we accumulated enough, we moved here to Colorado, and opened this very hotel twenty years ago."

We now stood in the main lobby with skylights above, and the man gazed upwards, proud of his achievements. He continued, "I have always been a people person, and wanted to surround myself in an environment where I would be able to meet good people and hear their stories, just like yours."

He looked around at the hanging artwork of mountain landscapes that mirrored the incredible panoramic views just outside the doors. I could see him reflecting on the choice he made over twenty years ago, proud of everything he had accomplished.

He said, "This hotel is not an over-the-top dream, but one where my wife and I can wake up every day feeling satisfied with what we are doing with our lives." He smiled after evaluating his life.

The hotel was not one of luxury with fifty-foot ceilings over a grand lobby and giant stuffed grizzly bears. But it was aimed, successfully, at travelers like Marisa and me.

The man explained that owning his own business had its ups and downs, and at times it was a real struggle to stay upright financially. But they were doing this for themselves, and every day was their own success story, every dollar was earned with satisfaction. The goal had never been to become rich, but to stay motivated and wealthy with a daily gratification money cannot purchase.

The tiny exhales of breath produced by each word he spoke were the equivalent of slowly blowing on an ember embedded in dry straw eagerly waiting to ignite. Each sentence bellowed the fire deep within Marisa and me.

He could not have been blunter in urging us to break free of the daily grind and to do something together that would satisfy our souls.

"Success or failure, it will bond you in ways unimaginable," he continued after thinking for a moment. "It will create the perfect environment for teamwork, problem solving, and finding out so much more about not only your soulmate, but who you are as individuals. Those are the real ingredients of happy people, happy marriages, and happy lives."

There was excitement in his voice for us, our future together, and what we could accomplish.

As we fully checked in, our unexpected muse bid us a good evening and good luck with the choices we would make.

"Just do it, guys, live your dreams. All you have is this one chance," he proclaimed as he disappeared behind the corner of the hallway.

Marisa turned to me and grabbed my arm with a smile. "I want us to be happy just like him and his wife. Find our calling and love every second of our life together," she said, inspired by not only the man's words, but the actions he took to achieve his goals.

"That guy was pretty enlightening. He needs to write the little blurbs in fortune cookies," I said in awe. "Maybe he's the reincarnation of Buddha or something. I feel all warm and fuzzy just listening to him."

As Marisa and I made our way back to the bike to unpack, we stood in the parking lot, digesting what we had just heard while taking in our new setting.

The sun was now at an angle that illuminated everything in sight with a golden hue. There were massive clouds that bloomed into white cauliflower patterns against a deep blue sky. The sun seemed to select random clouds and fill them with deep reds, yellows, and oranges, while leaving other manifestations of collected water alone to display their natural pure white.

"Let's do it," Marisa broke the silence in a tone that seemed to define our future. "You said the world, that you wanted to ride across the world. Let's explore it together."

I was shocked, thrilled. This couldn't have gone better. "So, you're saying you want to save as much as we can, quit our jobs, and just wing it as nomads?" I asked, unsure of her reaction despite her statement.

"I want to marry you and explore the wild frontiers of the world with the love of my life," she said with a smile. "Everything between now and that end result will only be to ensure that it happens."

"Mr. and Mrs. Notier exploring the world's frontiers. Notier's frontiers. That sounds nice," I said.

"Let's do it," Marisa repeated.

"There's also the possibility of this turning out to be Mr. and Mrs. Notier living in their parent's basement if we quit our jobs and fail to launch," I stated.

"That won't happen. I know we can do this," she urged.

"We could also get yellow fever and—"

"I know, Mr. Morbid," she interrupted. "It can end in a thousand different destructive ways. But it could also be the most exciting and gratifying thing we choose to do in our lives."

"Then it's official," I declared. "Let's do the most irresponsible yet rewarding thing we could ever possibly do. Let's do it. Let's explore the world together."

We each grabbed a pannier and took them into our room. That night, we laid on the bed and drifted to sleep with a full dose of inspiration for a brand-new path on life's many available roads.

##

Epilogue

Marisa and I were sold. We knew that small excursions on our summer breaks would not be enough to satisfy what we now envisioned ourselves capable of.

We had not even finished the trip at hand and were already calculating on how we could achieve a journey across the world. We had jumped from a three-week vacation, to the planning of a three-year expedition. There was a lot of research to be done, but we had time.

The list of gear needed grew ten-fold from my last brainstorm. Heated gear, rain gear that actually functioned as a water repellent, proper jackets with vents and basic armor, a better intercom system, actual motorcycle boots, and a full-face modular helmet for each of us were just a few of the items topping the list.

This was going to get expensive fast. I didn't have any idea how much it might cost to ship the bike around different impassable sections of the world, or across oceans, but I knew we needed as much money as we could possibly save. When the time was right, it would be enough.

As Marisa and I continued our trip around the Rocky Mountains, we successfully navigated through some of the highest roads in the continental United States. We hiked into and around the giant peaks that made up Rocky Mountain National Park. The trip had proved that we could tolerate each other for an extended amount of time and survive purely on what we could pack onto the KTM.

The journey had been a success, and as we walked back through the door to our home, all grimy and exhausted, we felt that we were no longer the same people who had left just nineteen days prior. Now our dream was in motion, and whether it was going to turn out for better or worse, we were jumping into the deep end.

Eleven of our twelve eggs all in one basket; a high-risk, but high-reward scenario. They say dangerous snakes are the most vulnerable while feeding; the same would be true in the initial consumption of our dream.

But we were willing to take that chance.

Author's Note:

Marisa and I have now been on the road since August of 2017.

Please follow us as we embark on an adventure of a lifetime at:

www.notiersfrontiers.com
www.facebook.com/notiersfrontiers
www.instagram.com/timnotier
www.youtube.com/notiersfrontiers

Take a look at our other titles that are available on Amazon:

2Up and Overloaded: Chicago to Panama

Blood, Sweat, and Notiers: Colombia to Ushuaia

"Live your dreams. All you have is this one chance."
– Wisest man I have ever met.

Please leave a review on Amazon!

Printed in Great Britain
by Amazon

75641495R00092